C000202657

DRINK TALKING

100 years of alcohol advertising

PUBLISHED BY MIDDLESEX UNIVERSITY PRESS

SERIES INTRODUCTION

The twentieth century saw the advertising industry become a dominant driving force in Western culture. It was the engine of capitalism, directed political destinies and even influenced international conflict and military victories by means of propaganda. Advertising has become a defining element in our lives and culture, holding a mirror to our social history, values and aspirations.

'The historians and archaeologists will one day discover that the advertisements of our time are the richest and most faithful daily reflections that any society ever made of its entire range of activities' (McLuhan, 1964, p.247)

This book is one of a series which describes the history of twentieth-century printed advertising. Each publication focuses on a different product. Most illustrations for this series come from The Library of Historic Advertising (LHA), an extensive collection of twentieth-century printed advertisements owned by Middlesex University and housed in the archives at their Cat Hill campus, London.

CONTENTS

Introduction

By 1999, the value of the British alcohol industry was £32.5 billion. Throughout the twentieth century, millions were spent each year on advertising its product. By 2001, the figure had risen to £181.3 million, £42.7 million of which was spent on beer, and lesser amounts on spirits and wine. Practically all the brands illustrated in this book are owned by the three major multinationals: Diageo, InterBev and Pernod Ricard. These companies spend such huge amounts on advertising for three main reasons: firstly to increase their market share, including increasing sales of new products through the establishment of a brand identity; secondly to remind people about their brands, many of which have been around for centuries, especially brands of whisky ILLUSTRATION I, gin and beer; lastly to encourage consumers to remain loyal to their brands in a very competitive market.

ILLUSTRATION I

1905

There's always a vacancy for a Double Diamond when things seem a bit empty. It works overtime to restore flagging morale, and puts a little more drive into life. An input of Double Diamond doubles your output of good cheer!

A DOUBLE DIAMOND
works wonders

IND COOPE'S **DOUBLE DIAMOND** BREWED AT BURTON

ILLUSTRATION 2

Punch, 1952

ILLUSTRATION 3

GQ, 1999

This brief history of twentieth-century printed advertising of alcoholic drinks covers advertisements of a selection of beers ILLUSTRATION 2, spirits (especially whisky, gin and vodka), champagnes, liqueurs ILLUSTRATION 3 and to a lesser extent wines (which didn't become a popular drink until the 1970s). The brands are either of British origin or those brands from abroad which have been advertised in the British press. American brands such as Budweiser are excluded.

This book will explore the rich iconography of alcohol advertising during the twentieth century and will look at patterns of consumption through descriptions of some famous, even iconic, advertising campaigns. Socio-economic factors and changes in lifestyles reflected in these advertising campaigns tend to emphasise the apparent health-giving benefits of certain products, the targeting of specific demographic groups such as women and young people, the importance of the Christmas market representing a disproportionate percentage of the whole spirit business and the promotion of alcohol to celebrate special occasions. The book also looks at the advertising of luxury products such as champagne ILLUSTRATION 4 to targeted audiences, the influence of supermarkets, the development of the lager market in the second half of the century linked to the rise in tourism, drinks companies increasingly sponsoring sporting activities and, in terms of the advertisements themselves, the specific changes in advertising techniques.

Mention will be made of the Campaign for Real Ale (CAMRA) set up in 1971 as well as the Portman Group, established in 1989 by Britain's leading drinks producers to promote responsible drinking through a voluntary code of practice[1], and its drink awareness campaigns. The views of this latter group and others like Alcohol Concern on the dangers to health of excessive drinking will be referred to later. In contrast to the campaigns of the drinks companies promoting their products are the government's anti-drink driving advertisements from the second half of the century.

This book follows the story of alcohol advertising up to the end of the twentieth century when the demand for tighter regulations and Internet competition have both had a significant impact on the printed alcohol advertisement.

1 The voluntary code of practice governing alcohol advertising is based on a number of core principles and prohibits any advertising which: targets young people under the age of 18; implies that alcohol can make you more socially or sexually attractive; encourages irresponsible drinking habits, especially binge-drinking; suggests any association with illicit drugs; or promotes the alcoholic strength of a drink.

ILLUSTRATION 4

1961

pop goes the Piper... *no wonder the French never drink water*

PIPER-HEIDSIECK CHAMPAGNE AVAILABLE IN PIPER BRUT 1953 VINTAGE • PIPER EXTRA DRY NON-VINTAGE • CUVEE DES AMBASSADEURS • PIPER PINK • RENFIELD IMPORTERS, LTD., N.Y.

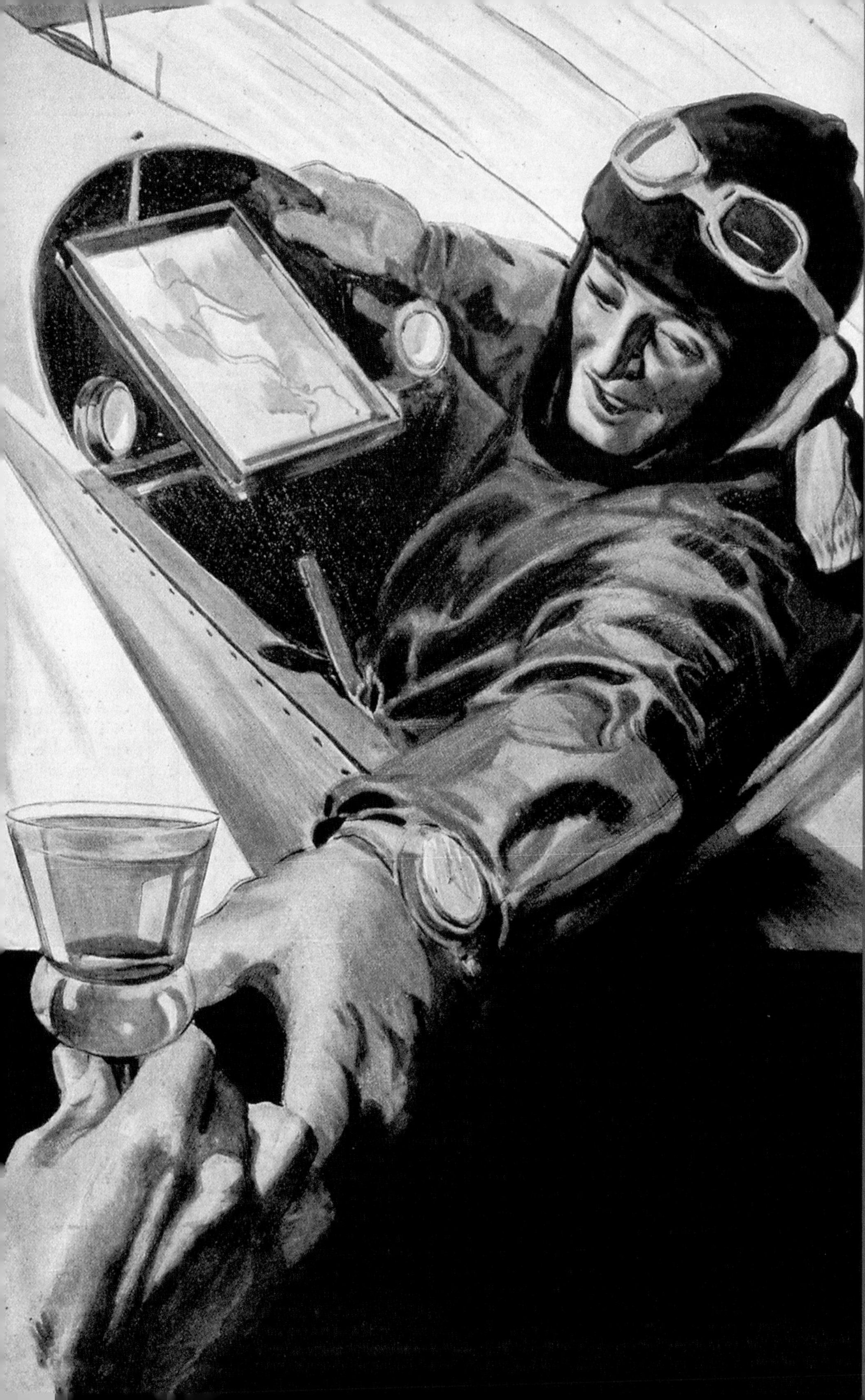

Chapter 1

1900–1930

The water of life

Beer has been drunk in Britain for centuries as an alternative to water, which remained largely unsanitary and unsafe until late Victorian times. Beer was consumed by all strata of society as an accompaniment to meals and, in some cases, was given as part payment for work done, usually to manual and agricultural workers. However, by the start of the twentieth century, beer had become associated with the poorer members of society.

During the first twenty years of the century, the majority of breweries were still local and their products were consumed by a local populace to whom there was no need to advertise. The few advertisements of the period 1900 to 1910 appear only in licensed trade publications such as the *National Guardian*, organ of the Scottish licensed trade. Here Tennent's (founded 1740) advertises to the trade its award-winning beer using its T trademark **ILLUSTRATION 5,** whilst Allsopp's proudly displays its royal warrant, stating that its ales, stouts and lager are unsurpassed **ILLUSTRATION 6**. Another reason for the existence of few advertisements is that the majority of British breweries owned their own chains of public houses (tied houses), thus guaranteeing both the distribution and sales of their products.

One theme which runs throughout the history of advertising alcohol is that beer and spirits have health-giving powers. An early example of beer's health benefits can be seen in an advertisement for Barrett's Stout for

ILLUSTRATION 5

National Guardian, 1908

ILLUSTRATION 6

National Guardian, 1908

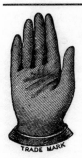

ILLUSTRATION 8

National Guardian, 1911

invalids **ILLUSTRATION 7**. The doctor is about to administer the stout to the patient whilst another young woman declares 'It saved my life'. Many alcohol products were endorsed openly by doctors and other medical personnel and stout was promoted for sick people and nursing mothers as late as the 1960s.

Some of the larger breweries did advertise in the trade press for export purposes. Carlsberg, founded in 1847 in Denmark and named Carlsberg ('Carl's hill') after the founder's son Carl and the hill on which the brewery was built, advertised its lager beer in a May 1911 edition of the *National Guardian*. The image shows the Danes delivering the exported beer to all parts of the world

including the countries of the Pacific **ILLUSTRATION 8**. The same year, in another advertisement showing men in uniform over the years, Bass is described as 'the drink of the Empire'. Bass's distinctive red triangle trademark of 1855 symbolises the company's long history and its quality.

At the beginning of the last century, spirit companies were heavily promoting their luxury products in the press to the wealthier members of society. During this same period many brands such as Hennessy, Martell and Dewar's became household names. Although brandies, like beers and whiskies, were considered to have health-giving properties, these two advertisements have very

MARTELL'S THREE STAR BRANDY.

ILLUSTRATION 10

The Graphic, 1903

ILLUSTRATION 9

1901

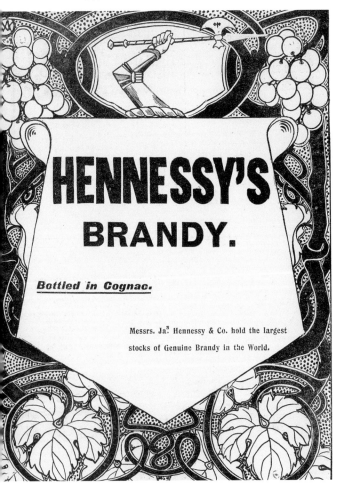

straightforward messages, promoting their products as symbols of extravagance and good taste. Hennessy's with its detailed border design claimed to hold the 'largest stocks of Genuine Brandy in the World' **ILLUSTRATION 9**, whilst Martell's 1903 advertisement is text only **ILLUSTRATION 10**. The effectiveness of this advertisement depends upon the 'three star' implying high quality. The health benefits of another contemporary product, Dubonnet, were asserted in an advertisement from the same year **ILLUSTRATION 11** including the advice to give children 'Half a wine-glass before each meal'!

The consumption of brandy declined during this period due to increased levels of excise duty, the spread of the phylloxera insect and the rise of competition from whiskies, the sales of which continued to increase due in large part to intensive advertising in the national press. Dewar's, founded in 1846, was one company which used advertising to keep its name at the forefront of whisky sales and its customers loyal **ILLUSTRATION 12**. 'The Beverage that Benefits' advertisement is an exquisite typographical etching.

Another whisky distillery, founded by John Walker in 1820, launched its Johnnie Walker brand in 1908. The

DUBONNET TONIC WINE

IS INVALUABLE FOR

Influenza, Headache, Loss of Appetite, Debility, Depression,

POVERTY OF BLOOD, PHYSICAL FATIGUE, DIGESTION, &c.

For CHILDREN—Half a wine-glass before each meal.
For ADULTS—One wine-glass before each meal.

Can be obtained from all Chemists, Wine Merchants, Grocers' Stores, Hotels, Bars, &c.

Price 2s. 8d. per Large Bottle.

Order locally, but if any difficulty in obtaining DUBONNET TONIC WINE, write to the
SOLE AGENTS FOR THE UNITED KINGDOM AND COLONIES—

INGRAM & ROYLE, Ltd., 26, Upper Thames St., London, E.C.,

who will forward one dozen bottles on receipt of 32s.

ILLUSTRATION 11

The Graphic, 1903

ILLUSTRATION 12

The Graphic, 1905

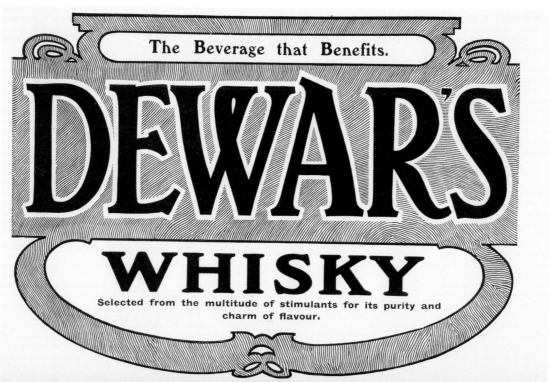

The Beverage that Benefits.

DEWAR'S WHISKY

Selected from the multitude of stimulants for its purity and charm of flavour.

ILLUSTRATION 13

The Illustrated London News, 1909

ILLUSTRATION 14

The Graphic, 1910

image on the bottles still remains that of a man with white trousers, morning coat and top hat along with the slogan 'Born 1820 still going strong'; the earliest advertisements, pen and ink drawings featured personifications of Johnnie Walker.

A 1909 advertisement **ILLUSTRATION 13** is an early example of a drinks company increasing the amount of its advertising in the run up to Christmas, when large percentages of its total annual sales were made. The scene resembles Dickensian times with the bountiful Johnnie Walker bringing seasonal cheer to the poor family with a box of his high-quality whisky. In Scotland, the New Year rather than Christmas has traditionally been the country's main celebration, as illustrated in an Usher's advertisement of 1 January 1910 **ILLUSTRATION 14**. The clever play on the company's name connects the whisky

ILLUSTRATION 15
Punch, 1913

DEWAR

Joseph Simpson, R.B.A.

Copyright. *John Dewar & Sons, Ltd.*

WALLACE

This Picture is the Sixth of a Series of colored Portraits of Famous Scots published by

JOHN DEWAR & SONS, L^{TD.}, Scotch Whisky Distillers, Perth & London

to the New Year personified as a baby. Dewar's ran a large series of etchings of Portraits of Famous Scots in *Punch* between 1913 and 1914, associating the whisky with strong Scots such as William Wallace **ILLUSTRATION 15**, famous for his height and strength and his defence of Scotland against the English.

During the First World War, with consumption of beer falling and that of spirits rising, the coalition Government of Lloyd George, dominated by the Liberals with their tradition of temperance, took the opportunity to control the sale and consumption of all alcohol. Its aims were to improve the fitness of the armed forces, reduce the

DEWAR'S

Keeps you Flying

ILLUSTRATION 16

Punch, 1914

ILLUSTRATION 17

The Illustrated London News, 1915

incidence of drunkenness of workers in heavy industries, including armaments, and thereby improve national efficiency. In 1915, whilst Minister of Munitions, Lloyd George stated that 'drink is doing more damage in the war than all the German submarines put together' (Burnett, 1999, p.132). That year he raised the duty on spirits from 14s 9d per gallon in 1914 to 29s 6d. Together with shortages of grains and sugar, this led to a huge decline in the consumption of spirits from 35 million gallons in 1914 to 15 million gallons in 1918. Additional legislation forcing distilleries to keep their whisky in bond for three years led to further shortages but ironically increased company profits. The government also passed the Defence of the Realm Act, which established a Central Control Board. This restricted the opening hours of the public houses to 5.5 hours per day (formerly 19.5) resulting in a massive decline in spirit and beer consumption.

Despite all these restrictions and a paper shortage, a few alcohol producers did continue their advertising as part of their patriotic duty as well as attempting to keep their products known. Just after the outbreak of the War, Dewar's produced an advertisement showing a flyer having a nip of whisky **ILLUSTRATION 16**, which was intended to boost morale. Although at that time still a local west country company, Bulmer's advertised its cider by combining the patriotic coupling of Union Jack and female worker with the traditional claim of health-giving properties **ILLUSTRATION 17**. In December 1915, the

THE WHITE WINE OF ENGLAND.

BULMER'S CHAMPAGNE CIDER

The Great National Beverage

Made exactly under the same process as Champagne, and considered by many to equal the most expensive Continental Wines, with this difference, that its properties are really beneficial to the health and ward off Gout and Rheumatism.

Cooling, Restful, Refreshing.

Wholesale London Agents :—
FINDLATER, MACKIE, TODD & CO., Ltd.
LONDON BRIDGE, S.E.

Write to the Makers to-day for FREE ILLUSTRATED BOOKLET.

H.P. BULMER & CO., HEREFORD.

Also Makers of the popular "Bull Brand" and Draught Ciders.

Born 1820—
still going strong.

THE TORONTO RITZ

CANADIAN A.S.C.

JOHNNIE WALKER: "You get your letters home, censored, eh?"

CANADIAN: "Yes, but we just put, 'like Johnnie Walker,' then those at home know we are 'still going strong!'"

JOHN WALKER & SONS, LTD., SCOTCH WHISKY DISTILLERS, KILMARNOCK.

ILLUSTRATION 18
The Illustrated London News, 1915

You can't tax Whisky

YOU can only tax people who consume whisky You can't tax any inanimate thing You ca[n] tax people

It is not whisky that pays the duty It is you If you drink beer you pay the beer tax If you drink wine you pay the [...]
If you drink whisky you pay the whisky tax

Very unfairly the man who drinks whisky pays a tax out of proportion to the man who drinks beer or wine

In the end Scotsmen will get this put right Most Scotsmen drink whisky and will not stand an injustice of this kind [...] effectively protesting

The duty on a bottle of whisky is 5/10 The duty on a bottle of port is 1/2½

A good "Home" industry can be killed quickly by this kind of blundering

Apart from its value in the home market, Whisky has an important "Export Value." It brings back food and raw mat[erial] our workers

Haig & Haig say this

Haig & Haig Five Stars Scots Whisky

IN the Home Market I am very scarce owing to Government restrictions No new accounts can be opened at present

MY famous contents are exported in this bottle
Africa is calling for me
India is calling for me
Ceylon is calling for me
Egypt is calling for me
ARE YOU?

HAIG & HAIG LTD.
HEAD OFFICE: 57 SOUTHWARK STREET, LONDON, S.E.1

ILLUSTRATION 19
Punch, 1919

Johnnie Walker used its slogan to boost morale amongst the troops in the trenches **ILLUSTRATION 18.**

After the end of the war, the restrictions remained in place with the passing of the Licensing Act 1921. One company which took great exception to the continued high duty on whisky was Haig – and it said as much in its advertisements **ILLUSTRATION 19.** In 1919, rates of duty had been expected to be cut but instead were maintained; and when the 1921 legislation was enacted, the Haig brand's vitriolic attacks continued unabated **ILLUSTRATION 20.** Two factors adding to the misery of whisky producers during the 1920s were the eventual take over by Distillers Company Ltd (DCL) of the majority of independent Scottish distilleries and the loss of the export market to the United States during its years of prohibition, 1920 to 1933.

ILLUSTRATION 20

Punch, 1921

Not Yet

❡ Some of us thought that we were going to get free of Government controls but, in spite of the need for it, it appears that we are NOT YET going to get our way.

❡ We are making money on our Export business and losing money on our Home business.

❡ We can only go on doing unprofitable business up to a point. With duty at 8/5½ per bottle the control price of 12/6 per bottle is *not enough* for a bottle of the quality that we are selling.

❡ We will not reduce the quality in order to make a profit in the Home Market. The only alternative left is to send our Whisky to the markets that appreciate quality and will pay for it.

❡ Will the public please note that it is not reluctance on our part to sell in the Home Market. It is (as the ex-Chancellor of the Exchequer said—in effect—in his last Budget speech) that the "Home" duty makes it unprofitable to sell FINE Whisky in a market that is controlled.

❡ Perhaps the new Chancellor will see that, by lowering the duty or removing control (or both), he will get a lot more Haig & Haig money, and the public will be better pleased.

Haig & Haig Five Stars Scots Whisky

HAIG & HAIG · LTD · (Distillers since 1679)
57 SOUTHWARK STREET · LONDON, S·E·1

We are advertising only our Export Bottle at present. The Government controls the price of whisky so that there is a loss on each case sold in the Home Market.

ILLUSTRATION 21
Punch, 1924

Before its merger with Bass in 1927, Worthington's advertised its products in various ways. In a 1924 advertisement in *Punch* **ILLUSTRATION 21** the health benefits of the beer were again emphasised using the image of a man wearing a hat (signifying respectability whilst in the pub) holding a glass of Worthington's. Beer had always been considered a masculine drink which this stereotypical man reinforces. A couple of years later Worthington used cartoon humour linked to the football Cup Final to advertise its brand and persuade football fans to drink its beer **ILLUSTRATION 22**. This is an early example of the connection between alcohol and sporting activities – although here only by association, rather than by sponsorship. This advertisement also exemplifies the development of the use of humour in alcohol advertising.

At the very end of the 1920s, Guinness[2] launched its first advertising campaign in Britain. Until then the company had believed that the product sold itself and therefore did not need to be advertised. Nevertheless, with declining sales and stiff competition from beers sold in tied-houses (of which Guinness owned none), Guinness was forced to compete through advertising. The advertising agency chosen for the campaign was S.H. Benson, which subsequently held the contract for just over forty years. There have been only five advertising agencies in total responsible for Guinness campaigns to date. Guinness advertising campaigns have reached iconic status due in part to the 'values underpinning Guinness of power,

2 Guinness was founded in 1759 in Dublin and opened its first brewery in London in 1936. It is now brewed in more than fifty countries.

ILLUSTRATION 22

The Sketch, 1926

ACCORDING TO A ROUGH ESTIMATE THERE WILL BE 119,982 SPECTATORS AT THE CUP TIE ——

OF THESE 59,991 WILL SHOUT FOR MANCHESTER CITY ——

AND 59,991 FOR BOLTON WANDERERS

SOME WILL SHOUT IN THE WRONG PLACE ——

AND OTHERS AT THE WRONG TIME

I SWALLERED ME WHISTLE

AND A SMALL PROPORTION EITHER FROM FORCE OF CIRCUMSTANCE OR BRONCHIAL TROUBLE WON'T SHOUT AT ALL ——

BUT FOR ALL RANKS, SIDES AND NATIONALITIES THE FINAL SHOUT WILL BE ——

Worthington

THE DAILY CHRONICLE

BOOTH'S DRY GIN

Holbrook's SAUCE

No. 20,812   LONDON   THURSDAY, FEBRUARY 7, 1929   LEEDS   ONE PENNY

THIS IS THE FIRST ADVERTISEMENT EVER ISSUED

in a national paper to advertise

GUINNESS

For over 150 years the House of Guinness have been engaged in brewing Stout. By concentrating upon doing one thing well, they have produced a beverage which stands alone.

Fortunes have been spent in study and development, going right back to the production of the kind of Barley seed that will enable the farmers to grow the Barley that makes the most suitable malt to make the best Stout.

As the result of quality, and quality alone, the Guinness Brewery has grown to be by far the largest in the world

ITS GREAT PURITY
Guinness is made solely from Barley Malt, Hops and Yeast, and is naturally matured. No artificial colour is added; the colour of Guinness is due to the roasting of the Barley.

ITS HEALTH-GIVING VALUE
Guinness builds strong muscles. It feeds exhausted nerves. It enriches the blood. Doctors affirm that Guinness is a valuable restorative after Influenza and other weakening illnesses. Guinness is a valuable natural aid in cases of insomnia.

ITS NOURISHING PROPERTIES
Guinness is one of the most nourishing beverages, richer in carbo-hydrates than a glass of milk. That is one reason why it is so good when people are tired or exhausted.

 # GUINNESS IS GOOD FOR YOU

Image courtesy of Diageo

ILLUSTRATION 23
The Daily Chronicle, 1929

goodness and community' which 'through the years have never been loud and brash but always clever and careful, relevant painstaking and responsible' (Griffiths, 2005, p.104).

The first Guinness beer advertisement appeared in the *Daily Chronicle* newspaper of 7 February 1929 with the slogan 'Guinness is good for you' **ILLUSTRATION 23**. Like many other beer and spirits advertisements, this listed the benefits of consuming the product as 'its great purity', 'its health-giving value' and 'its nourishing properties'. In greater detail, the seven main reasons for drinking Guinness beer were that it was 'good for your – Strength – Nerves – Digestion – Exhaustion – Sleeplessness – Tonic effects and Blood'. These seven elements appeared in a poster of the same year, represented by seven glasses of stout **ILLUSTRATION 24**. This implied that like an apple a day, Guinness could keep the doctor away – something that would have appealed to the British population in the days before the establishment of the National Health Service (1948), which provided the first free health care in Britain. From this first advertising campaign, Guinness beer has been portrayed as a high-quality product with a big personality, an image that would be fully exploited in the following decades.

ILLUSTRATION 24

1929

Chapter 2

1930s

Guinness galore

At the start of the 1930s beer consumption was still at a low level, having fallen from 20.69 gallons per head per annum in 1920 to 10.73 gallons by 1932. This was due partly to the lasting effects of First World War legislation and the impact of the economic depression of the late Twenties and early Thirties; but it was also due to the change in lifestyles of the working-class population of Britain. Whereas traditionally the working-class man had spent a fair percentage of his wages on drinking beer in pubs, he and his family were spending more now of their disposable income on other activities such as going to the cinema, dancing, working on allotments, playing and watching sports, and even taking paid annual holidays.

This all led the Brewers' Society in 1933 to launch an advertising campaign with the slogan 'Beer is best', promoting beer with images of healthy sporting and recreational activities, to try to boost sales. An early example of this is one of a large series of sporting calendar advertisements produced for Worthington **ILLUSTRATION 25**. A collage of the main sporting events for part of June 1933 is shown with the advice to 'put down in your notebook the events which interest you. And while you are at it, put yourself down for a Worthington'. It is worth noting that the target audience here is working-class men, with a few of the sports being aspirational, such as polo and yachting.

THE WORTHINGTON SPORTING CALENDAR

JUNE, 1933
1st to 10th inclusive

1st **Racing.** Epsom Meeting.
Shows. Royal Tournament, Olympia. Royal Counties Agricultural, Bournemouth. Suffolk Agricultural, Bury St. Edmunds.
Yachting. Royal Thames Y.C., Southend-on-Sea.

2nd **Racing.** Epsom, "The Oaks."
Lawn Tennis. Oxford v. Cambridge, Oxford.
Yachting. Southend Town Regatta.

3rd **Racing.** Kempton Park. Southwell & Hexham Steeplechases.
Yachting. Blackpool & Fleetwood Y.C. Cruiser Race. R.M. Y.C. Whitsun Regatta, Poole.
Polo. Junior Colts Cup, Ranelagh.
Regattas. Richmond & Twickenham.
Shows. Royal Military Ceremony, Trooping the Colour, Horse Guards Parade.

5th **WHIT MONDAY.**
Racing. Hurst Park, Redcar and Wolverhampton Meetings. Hexham, Fontwell, Wetherby, Newport, Buckfastleigh, Bungay, Cartmel and Huntingdon Steeplechases.
Athletics. British Games, White City. United Harriers' Sports, Luton.
Yachting. Royal Temple Y.C., Ramsgate.
Lawn Tennis. Essex Championships, Southend-on-Sea.
Motoring. Brooklands Mtg.
Polo. Hurlingham v. Army. Ranelagh Open Cup. Sutton Smith Cup, Roehampton.
Shows. Royal Tournament, Olympia. Notts. Agricultural Society, Welbeck. Colchester Horse Show.
Croquet. Gentlemen's and Ladies' Championship and Mixed Doubles Championships, Roehampton.

6th **Racing.** Hurst Park, Redcar and Wolverhampton Meetings.
Shows. Three Counties Agricultural Society, Worcester. Royal Tournament, Olympia.
Yachting. Royal Norfolk and Suffolk Y.C., Oulton.

7th **Racing.** Manchester. Yarmouth and Mallow Meetings.
Shows. Essex Agricultural Soc., Rochford. Northants Agricultural Society, Kettering. Berks Bucks and Oxon Champ. Dog Show.
Athletics. London Athletic Club Evening Meeting.
Golf. Scottish Professional Championship, Lossiemouth.
Cricket. Somerset v. West Indies, Taunton.

8th **Racing.** Manchester Meeting. Yarmouth & Gowran Pk. Mtgs.
Shows. Royal Tournament, Olympia. Essex Agricultural, Society, Rochford. Richmond Royal Horse Show.

9th **Racing.** Man. & Gatwick Mtgs.
Shows. Leicestershire Agric. Show, Leicester. Royal Tournament, Olympia.
Yachting. Clyde Corinth. Y.C.

10th **Racing.** Man. & Gatwick Mtgs.
Athletics. Marathon Race, Windsor to White City, London.
Greyhound Racing. Grand National Final, White City.
Shows. Aldershot Milit. Tattoo. Richmond Royal Horse Show.
Polo. Ranelagh Open Cup Final. Sutton Smith Cup Final, Roehampton.
Golf. West Wales Championship, Swansea.
Cricket. Middlesex v. West Indies, Lord's.
Yachting. The Yachting World Trophy, Poole.

PUT DOWN IN YOUR NOTEBOOK THE EVENTS WHICH INTEREST YOU. AND, WHILE YOU'RE AT IT, PUT YOURSELF DOWN FOR A WORTHINGTON.

ILLUSTRATION 25

The Sketch, 1933

ILLUSTRATION 26

The Sketch, 1933

Here's Health

HEALTHY exercise is at its best with social comfort and mental relaxation in charming surroundings. For refreshment Whitbread's Pale Ale is a beverage that is at once wholesome in its constituents and invigorating in effect.

It is sold all the World over and keeps its brilliance and fine flavour in all climates.

WHITBREAD'S PALE ALE

Issued by Whitbread & Co., Ltd., Gray's Inn Road, London, W.C.1.　　　　I.P.S.

Many breweries continued to promote their products as having health-giving benefits. A Whitbread's advertisement of 1933 **ILLUSTRATION 26** probably targeted the middle-classes. The setting is a social club where members can swim and then have drinks with their friends and fellow club members. Another Whitbread advertisement, 'Your advantage' of 1937 **ILLUSTRATION 27**, continued the link between sport and

Your Advantage

Whether you are a fierce devouring tiger or a mild lolloping rabbit at tennis, you are on equal terms when it comes to refreshment after the match.

There is nothing so cooling or invigor=ating as a glass of Whitbread's Pale Ale — and it keeps its brilliance and flavour in all climates and all conditions.

BREWED AND BOTTLED ONLY BY WHITBREAD & CO. LTD. LONDON, E.C.1

ILLUSTRATION 27

The Illustrated London News, 1937

beer but added a touch of sexual allure. The woman is seated in the umpire's chair, looking down on the male tennis player giving her the advantage of 'going for a drink'.

The same year Guinness followed suit in its 'Guinness is good for you' campaign **ILLUSTRATION 28** with a black and white advertisement in *Esquire* magazine giving 'sound reasons' for drinking Guinness. This whole decade of beer advertising is dominated by Guinness, whose campaigns led the field in originality, idiosyncrasy, humour and memorability. John Gilroy was instrumental in much of the success of the Guinness advertisement campaigns over the next three decades. Indeed, Gilroy was 'one of the most gifted and imaginative artists in the history of British advertising' (Sibley, 1985, p.46).

ILLUSTRATION 28

Esquire, UK, 1937

Image courtesy of *Diageo*

Sound Reasons for drinking Guinness

If all be true that I think,
There are five reasons we should drink;
Good brew...a friend...or being dry...
Or lest we should be by-and-by...
Or any other reason why!
Adapted from Henry Aldrich (1647-1710)

Had this genial poet lived today, or even in 1759, he would have found in Guinness the answer to all his requirements:

Good brew—Guinness is a natural brew. It contains barley malt, hops, yeast and water—nothing else. It is brewed in Dublin, slowly, in the cool of the year—aged for a twelvemonth—first in oak vats and then in Bottle.

A friend—Mutual enjoyment of Guinness is a natural way of making new friendships firm, and old friendships firmer. Or if you are alone, Guinness is a friend in itself.

Or being dry—Thirsty or not, the distinctive taste of Guinness has made more people enthusiastic about it than any other brew in the world. It is considered a compliment to be credited with a "Guinness palate."

Or any other reason why—There are many other reasons, but why list them? Your own enjoyment of Guinness is reason enough.

Guinness is enjoyed before or during meals, after exercise or when tired, and before retiring. You should be able to get it wherever you buy good beer or ale.

The story of Guinness since 1759: 66 pages, 44 illustrations. Write American Representative: A. Guinness, Son & Co., Ltd., Dept. 87-U, 501 Fifth Avenue, New York.

GUINNESS
IS GOOD FOR YOU
Since 1759

Copyright, 1937, by A. Guinness, Son & Co., Ltd.

ILLUSTRATION 29

1934

As part of the remit to increase take-home sales of Guinness beer, Gilroy and Bensons launched the 'Guinness for Strength' campaigns. One of the most famous examples of the campaign shows a man carrying an iron girder on his head, having gained strength from drinking a pint of Guinness **ILLUSTRATION 29**. The slogan was taken from the first of the seven reasons for drinking Guinness, namely 'strength', from the earlier Benson campaign to counterbalance the view that 'Guinness is good for you', which appealed more to women. Another example from 1937 is that of a lumberjack felling a very large tree having consumed a pint of Guinness **ILLUSTRATION 30**. This

ILLUSTRATION 30
1937

ILLUSTRATION 31
The Illustrated London News, 1931

slogan remained a regular part of the Guinness campaigns for the next thirty years, as did the black and green border with the red uppercase sans serif typeface.

The 'My Goodness, My Guinness' campaign was launched in 1935 using the first of many animals from Gilroy's menagerie, a sea-lion balancing a glass of Guinness beer on its nose. The most famous creature was the toucan, which started life as Gilroy's pelican but was changed by the copywriter (later a famous crime writer) Dorothy L. Sayers to a toucan. It was used throughout the years of Guinness advertising until pensioned off in 1982. The

demand for Guinness and other beers did rise after 1933, perhaps partly due to these advertising campaigns.

Like Guinness and the other beer producers, whisky companies continued to promote their products through advertising with even greater success. By the end of the decade, whisky was a very popular drink and made up seventy per cent of the total spirits market. A 1931 Highland Queen whisky advertisement **ILLUSTRATION 31** wittily illustrates the product's sense of its own importance and stature by showing a series of very tall buildings, towering above the tiny people and vehicles below.

ILLUSTRATION 32
The Illustrated London News, 1935

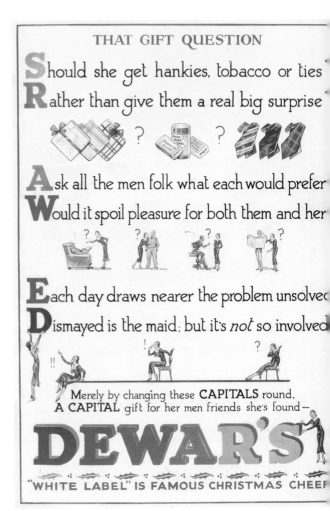

ILLUSTRATION 33
The Illustrated London News, 1936

Dewar's produced a series of colour advertisements marking special occasions in British history. This 1935 'Jubilee Spirit' advertisement celebrates King George V's Silver Jubilee **ILLUSTRATION 32** and links Dewar's prize-winning, royal-warranted high-quality whisky with summer holidays, and would have caught the mood of the British population. One assumes the presence of a soda siphon is to appeal to the overseas drinking market who read *The Illustrated London News*.

For Christmas 1936 Dewar's cleverly used acrostic verse and cartoon images representing the perennial seasonal alcohol producer's problem: how to entice consumers to read the advertisement and buy its product **ILLUSTRATION 33**. The bottle of whisky is not shown, simply the well-known brand name, featured twice – acrostically and at the bottom of the advertisement. One year later Dewar's Christmas advertisement featured the more traditional seasonal image of a Christmas cracker

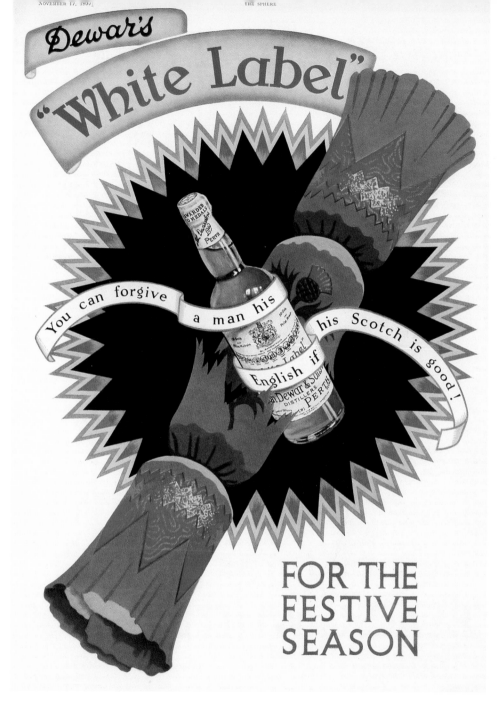

ILLUSTRATION 34

The Sphere, 1937

(with a clichéd thistle design) out of which emerges a bottle of Dewar's White Label **ILLUSTRATION 34**. The wording on the banner across the bottle, 'You can forgive a man his English if his Scotch is good', refers to the historic rivalry between the Scots and the English.

A Memorable Year

The Coronation

Floodlighting

Coronation Naval Review

Trans-Atlantic Air Service G-ADU...

CALEDONIA

Coronation Tattoo

Royal Ascot

FINE OLD SCOTCH WHISKY BLACK WHITE BUCHANAN GLASGOW & LONE

And now for

𝔠hristmas
and
"BLACK & WHITE"
SCOTCH WHISKY

SCOTCH WHISKY "BLACK & WHITE" SPECIAL BLEND OF CHOICE OLD SCOTCH WHISKY

ILLUSTRATION 35

The Sphere, 1937

Another example of whisky being associated with major national events is an advertisement for Black & White blended Scotch whisky, celebrating 1937 **ILLUSTRATION 35**.

Westminster Abbey is floodlit, trans-Atlantic flights have begun and King George VI has been crowned king after the abdication of his brother the year before.

Image courtesy of Diageo

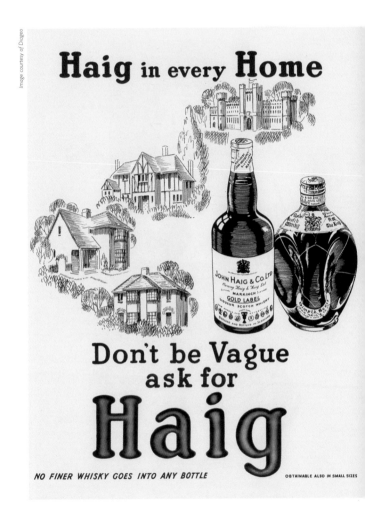

The Johnnie Walker brand prospered in the 1930s as whisky consumption grew. In contrast to the earlier Dickensian-style advertisement **ILLUSTRATION 13**, a 1936 advertisement uses a simple graphic device of black and white images of three men at a bar – two learners and one experienced drinker, the latter asking for a Johnnie Walker blended Scotch whisky by name **ILLUSTRATION 36**. The simplicity of the image enhances its appeal to men, and plays on their worries about asking for the right drink.

Having calmed down after its rant against the government's imposition of high duties after the end of the First World War, a 1937 Haig blended Scotch whisky advertisement provides an insight into how the company viewed its luxurious product **ILLUSTRATION 37**. The four

"It's the flavour"

86 PROOF

TEACHER'S
HIGHLAND CREAM
Perfection of Blended
Scotch Whisky

Teacher's warmth is welcomed, these days when cold winds bluster. It's mellow, mild and smooth. The brisk and hearty tang of it adds zest to fellowship. Teacher's is a good companion for the times you plan to remember.

Made since 1830 by Wm. Teacher & Sons, Ltd., Glasgow and London

SOLE AGENTS FOR THE UNITED STATES: Schieffelin & Co., NEW YORK CITY · IMPORTERS SINCE 1794

ILLUSTRATION 38
1937

homes shown in 'Haig in every Home' appealed to the lower social classes who aspired to succeed socially and financially, helped of course by the consumption of Haig's. The 'Don't be Vague ask for Haig' slogan was used for many years in the company's advertising campaigns and was at certain times as famous as those of Guinness.

Two other whisky advertisements from the period are for Teacher's, a blended whisky, and for the Famous Grouse, now one of the leading brands of blended whisky. Teacher's took its name literally in this 1937 advertisement showing the head and shoulders of a traditional teacher above a bottle of the brand **ILLUSTRATION 38**. The whisky is a 'good companion' whose flavour warms you up in cold Scottish weather.

On the other hand, a Famous Grouse advertisement of 1939 **ILLUSTRATION 39** contains somewhat clichéd images of heritage, Scottish heather, landed gentry and their sports. Apart from the unobtrusive line at its foot, you would not know it was a Christmas advertisement. The famous grouse takes centre stage without any mention of the Second World War, then three months old.

ILLUSTRATION 39

The Illustrated London News, 1939

ILLUSTRATION 40

The Illustrated London News, 1937

Champagne has always been considered a luxurious, expensive product to be consumed only on very special occasions. An advertisement for Lanson champagne is reproduced in black and white and does not have any images of celebration since it is aimed, as the copy states, at the connoisseur **ILLUSTRATION 40.** In complete contrast, an advertisement such as that for Piper Heidsieck champagne **ILLUSTRATION 4** is more exuberant and encapsulates celebrations.

By the late nineteenth century, gin was a very popular drink particularly amongst middle- and upper-class women in Britain who used it for mixed drinks, especially with tonic. It had managed by the twentieth century to re-image itself and lose its reputation as the 'calamitous curse of the urban poor, the Mother's ruin… the bathtub brew that rotted guts during American prohibition and the first resort of the miserable as the storm clouds of depression gathered' (Walton, 2006, p.408).

ILLUSTRATION 41

The Illustrated London News, 1935

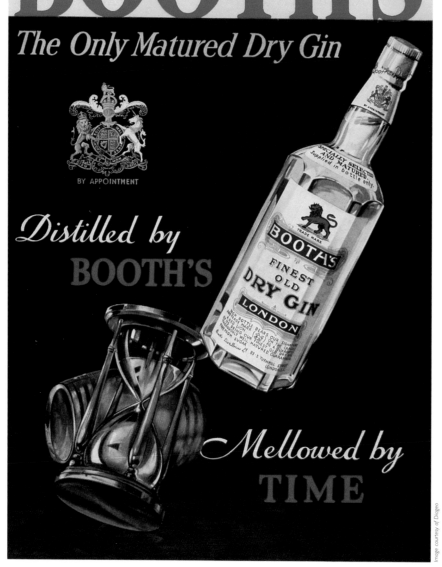

Image courtesy of Diageo

Booth's, founded in 1740, developed its dry gin in the 1870s and remains to this day a brand leader in London dry gin. A 1935 advertisement emphasised the gin's mature pedigree mellowed by time, represented by the image of an egg-timer. Graphically, it is a very beautiful advertisement using a palette of rich royal blue, red and gold and including a 'By Appointment' crest

ILLUSTRATION 41. A Gordon's gin advertisement of a few years later contains a picture of two women dressed to go out, one advising the other to drink a drop of gin as she is not feeling well **ILLUSTRATION 42**. Gordon's alleged medicinal properties are used here in a similar way to the health benefits associated with drinking Guinness, as mentioned earlier.

ILLUSTRATION 42

1938

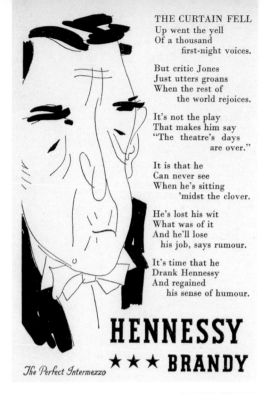

ILLUSTRATION 43

Theatre World, 1937

In a humorous advertisement for Hennessy three-star brandy featuring the glum face of a theatre critic, a poem targets critics and readers of *Theatre World* magazine, who may well have needed a drop of brandy after sitting though some performances **ILLUSTRATION 43**. A 1938 advertisement **ILLUSTRATION 44** shows how radically Martell had changed its advertising techniques since its 1903 advertisement **ILLUSTRATION 10**. Four vignettes of middle-class life in Britain in the late 1930s celebrate every occasion: men in coats and hats having a drink after work; friends at the end of dinner in a restaurant; a couple having dinner; and a man in a club drinking alone. The fashions, furnishings and traditions of the 1930s are all beautifully captured.

ILLUSTRATION 44

The Illustrated London News, 1938

ILLUSTRATION 45

Esquire, UK, 1936

Unlike brandy, Britain's first rums had traditionally been drunk by the working-classes and had strong associations with the Royal Navy. Nevertheless, the first advertisements for Bacardi rum appeared in 1933 and played heavily on its exotic Cuban origins. The aim of the advertisements was to establish the brand's superiority through being a cocktail in a tropical setting, at a time when foreign travel to such places as Cuba was the domain of the wealthy. In a 1936 advertisement **ILLUSTRATION 45** Bacardi dark rum is illustrated: the more famous white rum gained popularity later in the century. Two stylised, seated men dressed in suits and ties, in an exotic setting under a tropical sky, are being served by a stylish Latin American waiter holding the 'singing' Bacardi.

ILLUSTRATION 46

The Illustrated London News, 1934

ILLUSTRATION 47

1937

Other products with exotic origins included Martini & Rossi's dry and sweet vermouths, first advertised in Britain in the 1930s. The first of the two advertisements features the head of a middle-aged man, eyes closed, holding a top hat, wearing gloves and leaning over a very large Martini sign with the products centre stage **ILLUSTRATION 46**. The next advertisement contains very different imagery of men and women wearing swimming costumes or bathrobes, sitting and standing round a swimming pool suggesting enhanced physical and sexual attractiveness. The copy encourages them to drink Martini as a tonic to build themselves up after strenuous exercise. It is healthful, always 'right', the latter being an early use of the later famous slogan 'Martini: the right one' **ILLUSTRATION 47**.

Chapter 3

1940s

High spirits

Shortly after the outbreak of the Second World War, the government's Committee on Brewing and Distilling imposed strict controls on the production of alcohol, similar to those used during the 1914–1918 period. Despite this, beer consumption continued to grow. Whisky production was maintained during the first two years of the war in order to be exported to America in exchange for armaments and food. This arrangement ended in 1942 when America entered the war, causing grain shortages leading to a temporary closure of all Scottish distilleries. A shortage of newsprint and the consequent rationing of advertising resulted in a decline of whisky sales, making whisky a drink of the rich once the war had finished. Gin more or less disappeared from the shops during the war due to very high levels of excise duty.

Despite wartime paper and advertising rationing, beer companies continued to advertise their products in order to keep their names in the public domain whilst at the same time doing their bit for the war effort. A Worthington advertisement of February 1940 encourages consumers to 'smile and drink the beer' even in such adverse times. The wording and sentiment hark back to the First World War song 'Pack up your troubles in your old kit bag and smile, smile, smile' **ILLUSTRATION 48**. A Bass beer advertisement from a few weeks later in the same magazine appeals to women and makes absolutely no mention of the war **ILLUSTRATION 49**. One interpretation is that the company realised that, with the

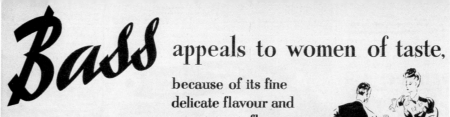

Bass appeals to women of taste,

because of its fine
delicate flavour and
energising influence

ILLUSTRATION 49

Picture Post, 1940

ILLUSTRATION 48

Picture Post, 1940

*A smile is as infectious as a yawn —
and much more valuable just now.
Do you remember the old poem:*

> " 'Tis easy enough to be pleasant
> When life flows along like a song
> But the man worth while is the
>   one who will smile
> When everything goes dead wrong . . ."

*So — smile. And if your courage flags
a little, put your troubles in their
place with a Worthington — brewed
for your good heart from the
smiling English fields.*

MORE POPULAR THAN EVER

In the Mess, in hotels, restaurants and bars—no less than in the home—the call is for Whitbread's superb Pale Ale.

Brewed from British hops and barley; appetizing, refreshing, stimulating; Whitbread's superb Pale Ale is more popular than ever.

WHITBREAD'S PALE ALE

BREWED & BOTTLED BY WHITBREAD & CO., LTD., LONDON, E.C.1

ILLUSTRATION 50
The Tatler and Bystander, 1941

men away at war, women would be left at home earning – and therefore possibly consuming beer! A 1941 advertisement for Whitbread's Pale Ale subtly refers to the war through its mention of 'the Mess', the place where service men and women ate and drank **ILLUSTRATION 50**.

The nondescript setting and low-key message contrast with those of Guinness which continued to use humour in its advertisements to raise morale. The S.H. Benson agency adapted two of its 1930s advertising slogans,

'Guinness for Strength' and 'My Goodness, My Guinness', for its wartime advertising campaigns. In a 1942 advertisement drawn by Gilroy, the 'Guinness for Strength' caption is combined with the government's slogan 'Dig for victory' **ILLUSTRATION 51**. The top part of the advertisement represents the government's exhortation to the British people to grow their own food as part of the war effort, whilst the main advertisement shows a man pushing an exaggeratedly large wheelbarrow laden with home-grown produce and a Guinness beer bottle in a basket on his head. Another

ILLUSTRATION 51

1942

Image courtesy of Diageo

GUINNESS FOR STRENGTH

Drawing by J. Gilroy

ILLUSTRATION 52

The Tatler and Bystander, 1943

ILLUSTRATION 53

The Tatler and Bystander, 1941

My Goodness — My GUINNESS

ILLUSTRATION 54

The Tatler and Bystander, 1944

Image courtesy of Diageo

"My Goodness — My Guinness"

G.E.1182.A

'Guinness for Strength' advertisement of 1943 makes reference back to the man carrying the iron girder on his head, adapted for wartime into a long gun barrel being carried on to a warship, an empty Guinness glass at one end **ILLUSTRATION 52**.

The 'My Goodness, My Guinness' slogan was adapted in a humorous way to show the threat posed by the war to Guinness drinkers (and by association, the British people) in a 1941 advertisement drawn again by Gilroy **ILLUSTRATION 53** and, three years later, in one drawn by H.M. Bateman[3] **ILLUSTRATION 54**. Never one to miss an advertising opportunity, Guinness targeted women who had once again become part of the workforce in the men's absence, as had happened during the First World War.

3 H.M. Bateman (1887–1970), cartoonist and caricaturist for many famous magazines, including *Punch*.

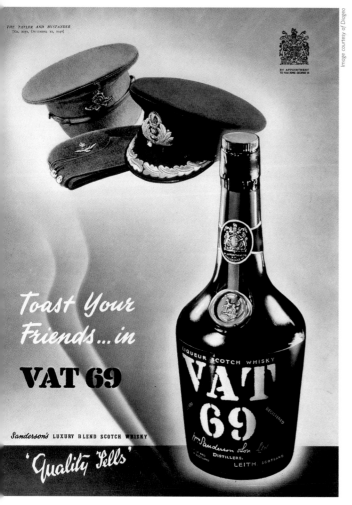

ILLUSTRATION 55
The Tatler and Bystander, 1940

Good work – good whisky

JOHNNIE WALKER
Born 1820 – still going str

ILLUSTRATION 56
The Illustrated London News, 1942

Until the closure of the whisky distilleries in 1942 a few companies produced advertisements in support of the war effort. A VAT 69 blended Scotch whisky bottle appears beside three caps representing the three main services, toasting friends in the run up to Christmas 1940, continuing the tradition of the large sales and advertising push at the festive season, despite the war **ILLUSTRATION 55**. An advertisement of 1942 for the Johnnie Walker brand makes its contribution to the war effort more

explicit by linking the successful launching of another British ship against all odds (at a time when British shipping was suffering heavy losses) with its excellent product **ILLUSTRATION 56** still going strong like the British. Even the Black & White blended Scotch whisky company, in a 1943 advertisement, reinforces the messages of making do, saving resources as part of the war effort, and ultimate victory. Although an American advertisement, the message applied equally to the British people **ILLUSTRATION 57**.

ILLUSTRATION 57

1943

ILLUSTRATION 58

The Illustrated London News, 1941

Image courtesy of Diageo

Blackie: "That storekeeper was sure glad when we said we'd carry our own bundles, Whitey."

Whitey: "He knows what it means to save trucks and tires — for Victory, Blackie!"

Can you take it? Then don't say "send it." Every package you carry saves trucks and tires for vital deliveries — to keep foodstuffs coming to the grocer and the dairy, to keep raw materials moving to factories. So don't go away empty-handed. Carry your own bundles — for Victory!

EIGHT YEARS OLD

A 1941 advertisement for Dewar's White Label whisky **ILLUSTRATION 58** shows normal life back home — two older professional-looking men (possibly in reserved occupations) are enjoying a glass of Dewar's with a game of darts in a pub after a hard day's work in the office. The intention would have been to remind the troops that normal life was still there to come home to. A similar

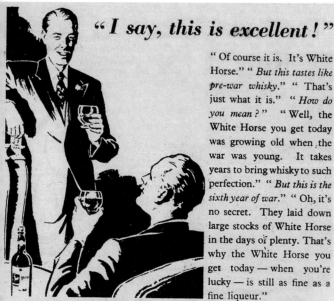

"*I say, this is excellent!*"

" Of course it is. It's White Horse." " *But this tastes like pre-war whisky.*" " That's just what it is." " *How do you mean?*" " Well, the White Horse you get today was growing old when .the war was young. It takes years to bring whisky to such perfection." " *But this is the sixth year of war.*" " Oh, it's no secret. They laid down large stocks of White Horse in the days of plenty. That's why the White Horse you get today — when you're lucky — is still as fine as a fine liqueur."

WHITE HORSE

MAXIMUM PRICES—*Bottles* 25/9 ; *Half-bottles* 13/6
as fixed by The Scotch Whisky Association.

ILLUSTRATION 59
Picture Post, 1945

You can replace the stopper — we can't

PLEASE be careful to screw the stopper back in place after the bottle is empty. These Bulmer screw stoppers are made of rubber, so by taking a little care you are helping the National ' Save Rubber Campaign.'

Bulmer's Cider

H. P. BULMER
& CO., LTD.
HEREFORD.

royds 53

ILLUSTRATION 60
Picture Post, 1943

image is shown in a 1945 advertisement as the war neared its end **ILLUSTRATION 59**. Since whisky has to mature for years before it is ready for sale, the White Horse brand stressed that its product was laid down before government's restrictions were applied, making it in short supply and therefore a luxury.

Another company doing its bit for the war effort was Bulmer's cider **ILLUSTRATION 60**, exhorting people to help with the government's campaign to Save Rubber. Despite the fact that Italy was at war with Britain, an advertisement for Martini appeared in a 1940 issue of the *Picture Post* emphasising again the still health-giving

properties of its product essential during wartime — though these two people look fairly relaxed about the war **ILLUSTRATION 61**.

The end of the war was celebrated in alcohol advertising, as in this Gilbey's brand advertisement for its gin and port **ILLUSTRATION 62** even though restrictions and rationing lasted long after the war and into the Fifties. In a 1946 colour advertisement for Bulmer's cider **ILLUSTRATION 63**, at a time when demand was outstripping supply, the woman appears more homely and healthy, out gardening but pausing to drink some cider made from home-grown British apples.

THE GAY-WAY TO HEALTH

Mr. & Mrs. OWEN NARES
enjoying a plain Martini Vermouth,
their favourite meal-time drink.

PLAIN MARTINI Vermouth is the ideal drink before or with the meal. This fine rich health-giving wine never leaves an unpleasant after-effect, for it is infused with rare aromatic herbs that tone up the stomach, heart, liver and kidneys. For the sake of your appetite, your digestion, your figure and your general health you should drink *plain Martini Vermouth* —Dry or Sweet.

MARTINI
Vermouth
Product of Martini & Rossi - Torino

DRY OR SWEET
DRINK IT NEAT

★ *Refuse Inferior Substitutes —*
look for the Martini label

ILLUSTRATION 61

Picture Post, 1940

ILLUSTRATION 63

John Bull, 1946

ILLUSTRATION 62

Picture Post, 1945

Post, June 30, 1945

HERE'S TO THE FUTURE!
HAPPY DAYS —
PEACE AND PROSPERITY
AND MORE

GILBEY'S
GIN AND
GILBEY'S PORT

Apples all the year round in
Bulmer's
Cider

PLEASE REPLACE STOPPER

BULMER'S
WOODPECKER
CIDER

Bulmer's is positively *made* of apples—2½ lbs. to EVERY FLAGON. Sorry we still can't supply all you need, but we do see that distribution is fair.

H. P. BULMER & CO., LTD. HEREFORD

Can You Settle This Dispute About Drinks?

French Attaché Asserts:
If a Bacardi Cuba Libre is not
the most refreshing, coolest
drink man has invented, parbleu!
. . . what is? Every sip makes
the taste tingle with delight!

Chilean Consul Claims:
Obviously a Bacardi Collins is for
the palate of discrimination.
Consider the crystal coolness of this
perfect summer drink. There is
no rival for a Bacardi Collins!

Looking at the subject coolly, we'd say
Bacardi wins in either case! Bacardi and
Bacardi alone is the perfect answer for
both a tingling Cuba Libre . . .
and a long, frosty Collins!

all nations agree — BACARDI

RUM . . . 89 Proof. Bacardi Imports, Inc., New York

ILLUSTRATION 64
1946

hen Hengest and Horsa staged their commando raid on the st of Kent, they selected Pegwell Bay because they thought name sounded so promising. Wouldn't they have been serker if they had known that they were missing Pimm's No. 1 : Original Gin Sling) by less than a couple of thousand years !

Pimm's No. 1
The Original Gin Sling

E MERCHANTS HAVE LIMITED SUPPLIES FROM TIME TO TIME AT 27/6 PER BOTTLE

AFTER MEASURING THE WOODS

they bowl along for a measure of

GILBEY'S GIN

ILLUSTRATION 66
1947

ILLUSTRATION 65
Punch Almanack, 1947

After the end of the Second World War there was a desire amongst nations to settle future differences peacefully and diplomatically, under the auspices of the newly established United Nations organisation. A 1946 Bacardi advertisement **ILLUSTRATION 64** alludes to the United Nations in its copy 'all nations agree' – though in this example it's to rum and not war! A black and white advertisement of 1947 for the Pimm's brand uses humour by showing two Vikings drinking on a British

beach **ILLUSTRATION 65**, with the bottom line indicating that rationing was still in force causing 'wine merchants [to] have limited supplies from time to time'. Gin, having virtually vanished during the war, reappeared in the late 1940s. A small advertisement for Gilbey's gin **ILLUSTRATION 66** in which two men are playing crown green bowling, a common sport of the working-classes at the time, employs wordplay on bowling terms and shows life in peace time getting back to normal.

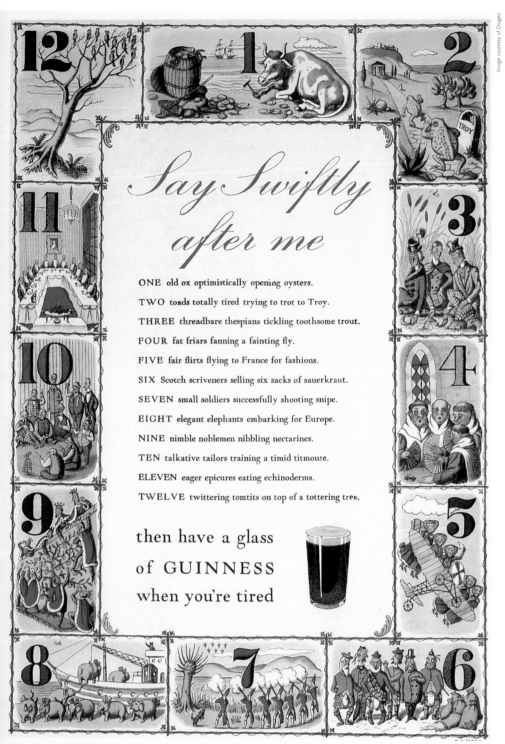

Say Swiftly after me

ONE old ox optimistically opening oysters.

TWO toads totally tired trying to trot to Troy.

THREE threadbare thespians tickling toothsome trout.

FOUR fat friars fanning a fainting fly.

FIVE fair flirts flying to France for fashions.

SIX Scotch scriveners selling six sacks of sauerkraut.

SEVEN small soldiers successfully shooting snipe.

EIGHT elegant elephants embarking for Europe.

NINE nimble noblemen nibbling nectarines.

TEN talkative tailors training a timid titmouse.

ELEVEN eager epicures eating echinoderms.

TWELVE twittering tomtits on top of a tottering tree.

then have a glass
of GUINNESS
when you're tired

ILLUSTRATION 67

1947

Benson's continued to produce humorous advertisements for Guinness, especially in high-quality magazines such as the *Tatler*. This very witty 1947 example, drawn by Antony Groves-Raines, is based on the Twelve Days of Christmas song adapted into a fiendishly difficult tongue twister **ILLUSTRATION 67**.

This decade of advertising alcohol is brought to an end with a 1949 advertisement for the Haig brand, which retains its pre-war optimism despite having suffered a massive sales drop during the war and a reduction in its market share after the war. Two bottles of Haig blended Scotch whisky are shown: a plain modern bottle next to the traditional dimpled shape. Their placement in an oyster shell associates the luxurious pearl with the drink **ILLUSTRATION 68**. The Christmas card looks incongruous in the foreground of this beach scene, especially given that this dates from the leaner post-war years.

ILLUSTRATION 68
Country Life, 1949

Chapter 4

1950s

Beer and bubbles

The 1950s in Britain was a period of post-war economic recovery and prosperity beginning with the 1951 Festival of Britain. With the cessation of grain rationing in 1953 and the end of full rationing in 1954, the consumption of spirits and beer began to climb back to its pre-war sales levels.

In the first half of the Fifties, the Guinness brand continued to dominate the beer advertising market with advertisements like this black and white image from 1950 **ILLUSTRATION 69**, re-using a slogan from the Thirties. But other breweries were beginning to emulate Guinness's national marketing and advertising campaigns.

Bass produced a vast series of 'This England' advertisements **ILLUSTRATION 70**. They were all photographs of different parts of the country, harking back to the pre-war days and thus emphasising the return to the good old way of life. At first glance, it's difficult to see what the product is until you find the words 'Bass' or 'Worthington' in the text. It must be assumed that after the first couple of advertisements, readers would quickly have associated the drink with the picture.

March 29 1950

Family Group

**THERE'S NOTHING LIKE
A GUINNESS
WHEN YOU'RE TIRED**

ILLUSTRATION 69

Punch, 1950

This England . . .

Tarn Hows — Lake District.

OF ALL the Englands that go to make this England, that of "the lakes" differs perhaps more than all. And each of us will think his favourite lake—studded maybe with little isles that fascinate the boy in us—to be the loveliest of all. Yet this is still England, bank and tree, cart-rut and sheltered farm, the common things of life proclaim it. And so it is, climber or walker or simple beauty-seeking tourist, that here too—your lungs filled with the crisp air, your coat sodden upon your back (for it can rain in these parts)—you will find another good thing common to English life . . . Your sunfilled Bass or Worthington, rich-brewed to soothe fatigue and keep your heart alift till dusk shall steal the beauty from your eyes.

ISSUED BY BASS AND WORTHINGTON, BURTON-UPON-TRENT, ENGLAND

ILLUSTRATION 70

1950

It's the appetising taste of Guinness that goes so well with food

WHAT A TREAT it is to eat with Guinness! How well it goes with the food that you love best. Creamy, refreshing, and delightfully clean in flavour, Guinness quickens the appetite and rounds off a meal.

HOW TO ENJOY YOUR T.V. MORE
in 2 lessons

1. When there is something special to watch, and people are coming home late, get a simple spread ready to eat round your set.

2. To make your simple spread simply delightful get in a few bottles of Guinness - it is always enjoyed a lot. And it's so good for you.

Image courtesy of Diageo

ILLUSTRATION 71
1955

Image courtesy of Diageo

'Thank you, Mike, for teaching me how good Guinness tastes!'

ILLUSTRATION 72
1957

The Fifties was also the decade when various drinks companies such as Mackeson, Whitbread, Campari and Babycham started targeting women as a separate market. Female spending power had begun to increase and it was no longer considered socially unacceptable for women to be seen alone in pubs.

One of the reasons Guinness decided to target women again (as it had done during the war) was that, despite spending a million pounds on advertising campaigns, a 1951 piece of market research had shown that its main market was older men, who by definition (literally) constituted a diminishing market share. At the same time as it embarked on advertising on commercial television in 1955, Guinness produced printed advertisements showing a man and a woman with meals on their laps, watching television and drinking Guinness beer **ILLUSTRATION 71**. The copy stressed the taste of

Some people prefer

MACKESON'S
STOUT

—*it's a matter of taste*

Generally, stout has a slightly bitter taste. But
Mackeson's mellow smoothness comes as a pleasing
change to many who take a rich, reviving glass
after the long day's housework is over.

Try it, and taste the difference!

BREWED AND BOTTLED BY **WHITBREAD**   27 BRITANNIA STREET, LONDON, W.C.1

ILLUSTRATION 73

Punch, 1950

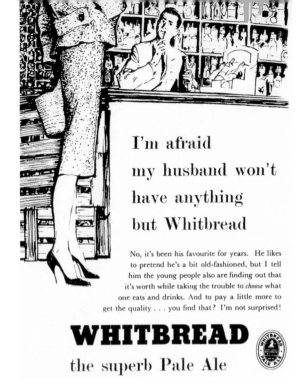

I'm afraid
my husband won't
have anything
but Whitbread

No, it's been his favourite for years. He likes
to pretend he's a bit old-fashioned, but I tell
him the young people also are finding out that
it's worth while taking the trouble to *choose* what
one eats and drinks. And to pay a little more to
get the quality . . . you find that? I'm not surprised!

WHITBREAD
the superb Pale Ale

ILLUSTRATION 74

1956

Guinness. Most people in the 1950s sat at a table to eat
their meals and this advertisement represents a major
social change in eating habits.

Another Guinness advertisement from two years later
shows a woman out having a drink with a male friend,
who has introduced her to the delights of Guinness beer.
The copy 'Thank you, Mike, for teaching me how good
Guinness tastes' **ILLUSTRATION 72** might not be so well
received in this century. Although the 'My Goodness, My
Guinness' crocodile poster on the wall behind the woman
was at first considered too 'sinister', its genial expression,
twinkling eye and crocodile tear proved a success and
sales of Guinness to women slowly began to rise.

Like the previous Guinness advertisement, a 1950
Mackeson's advertisement is also aimed at women, but
shows the woman in her domestic setting having a glass

of Mackeson's at home after a long day's housework is
over **ILLUSTRATION 73**. The contrast between these two
advertisements is immense in that this one reinforces the
stereotypical housewife image. Married women in the
1950s were expected to stay at home and bring up the
family. Mackeson's had been recommended for decades
for nursing mothers but here it is presented as socially
acceptable for all women to drink the product.

Women traditionally received regular housekeeping
monies, with which they not only bought the groceries
but also alcohol for home consumption. Women's
increased purchasing of alcohol, usually for their men, is
the subject of a 1956 advertisement for Whitbread's Pale
Ale **ILLUSTRATION 74**. The setting is an off-licence. The
headline demonstrates the brand loyalty for which all
companies strive, whilst the copy links the 'older husband'
with the young people's drinking habits.

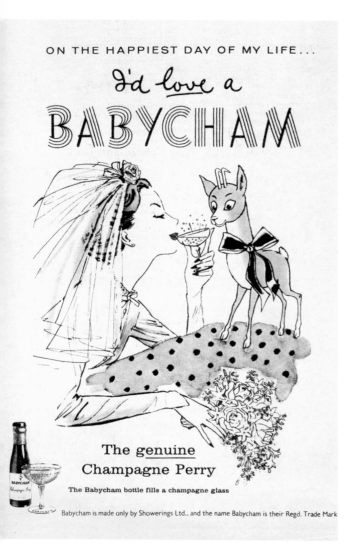

ON THE HAPPIEST DAY OF MY LIFE...

I'd love a

BABYCHAM

The genuine
Champagne Perry

The Babycham bottle fills a champagne glass

Babycham is made only by Showerings Ltd., and the name Babycham is their Regd. Trade Mark

AMERICANO
½ Jigger Bitter Campari, ½ Jigger Italian Vermouth, squeeze of lemon and cracked ice. Serve with or without Soda-Water (this is a very popular cold drink on the French Riviera).

CAMPARI SODA
I Jigger Bitter Campari in a tumbler with a good splash of Soda-Water. Serve very cold (this is how Campari is served in Rome).

NEGRONI (long drink)
Pour into a large tumbler one measure of Gin, a good portion of Bitter Campari and red Vermouth, add some ice and a good splash of soda. Serve with a slice of orange.

THE APERITIF

THESE discerning young people know a good thing at parties — they are drinking Campari. The waiter serves them with a knowledgeable smile; he knows that they have found **the** aperitif . . . . and he has found **two** connoisseurs.

CAMPARI

WITH VERMOUTH · WITH SODA · IN COCKTAILS & IN LONG

ILLUSTRATION 75

1959

ILLUSTRATION 76

The Illustrated London News, 1958

Babycham was one of the most famous advertising campaigns aimed at women of the decade. The product was invented by Francis Showering and was made from pears as a short, not-too-alcoholic drink for women who did not drink beer but could not afford whisky and other spirits. It was launched in 1953. Its slogan 'I'd love a Babycham' is still recognised by the baby-boomer generation, which fondly remembers the leaping fawn and the small bottle sufficient to fill one champagne glass **ILLUSTRATION 75**. A 1959 advert shows a woman drinking Babycham on her wedding day, indicating that it was as special as real champagne. Babycham's popularity was at its height in the 1960s.

May the generous hope of
peace and prosperity be the dominating
note of Her reign

ILLUSTRATION 77

The Queen, 1953

Another example of 'sophisticated' drinking habits is a 1958 Campari black and white advertisement showing two young women drinking cocktails. Their fashions look forward to the Sixties and the aspirational association with European travel – drinking Campari soda mixer as served in Rome – would have been clear at a time when the British considered anything Italian romantic **ILLUSTRATION 76**.

Drinks companies often ran special advertising campaigns to celebrate national occasions such as the coronation of Queen Elizabeth II. An advertisement for Booth's gin **ILLUSTRATION 77** appeared in *The Queen* magazine on the actual day of the coronation (3 June 1953). It shows an appropriately refined image of a female and male hand toasting her new majesty (the first use of EIIR), the silver platter and royal warrant denoting the high quality both of the product and its drinkers.

ILLUSTRATION 78

Picture Post, 1953

ILLUSTRATION 79

The Queen, 1954

At the opposite end of the class spectrum is this colourful, joyous, humorous cartoon of the British people outside Buckingham Palace watching the royal procession **ILLUSTRATION 78**. The pile of Double Diamond bottles provides the bowler-hatted man with the best viewing platform in the crowd thus making real the slogan that 'A Double Diamond works wonders'. Even the normally stern guardsman is smiling.

Champagne, the classic celebratory drink, is illustrated in a 1954 advertisement for Moët & Chandon **ILLUSTRATION 79**. The advertisement contains vignettes of the great and gay social occasions, including the coronation of the previous year, and the royal warrant of the late King George VI.

Towards the end of the Fifties, British breweries such as Watney's were having to compete increasingly with lager products imported from abroad such as Carlsberg (Denmark) and Carling (Canada). Watney's two main beers – Red Barrel, launched in the Thirties, and its Brown Ale – continued their advertising campaigns as illustrated in a 1957 Brown Ale advertisement **ILLUSTRATION 80**. The advertisement shows a traditional pub setting, with games of darts and beer, and oozes masculinity. In contrast, a John Smith's advertisement for its Magnet ale shows a glass of beer and a glamorous woman looking out enticingly at the male readers.

ILLUSTRATION 80

The Illustrated London News, 1958

When the choice is Lager—

The Call is for

Carlsberg

Lager at its best!

The pleasures of Carlsberg are widely trumpeted. Why? Because Carlsberg entertains the palate with sparkling pleasure . . . because it's a tingling top-liner in taste, straight from Denmark, where it's brewed and bottled to become appreciated *everywhere*.

Remember, ladies — Carlsberg Lager is guaranteed absolutely pure-brewed, entirely without sugar or chemicals.

★ TRY CARLSBERG DANISH PILSNER OR CARLSBERG LAGER EXPORT DE LUXE

Reproduced courtesy of Carlsberg UK Limited

ILLUSTRATION 81

1956

Carlsberg was exporting its lager to Britain with the aim of denting the home-grown beer market. In the British film *Ice Cold in Alex*, on reaching Alexandria, John Mills asks the barman to set up four ice-cold Carlsberg lagers. In a 1956 advertisement **ILLUSTRATION 81**, a hip young couple ask for a lager 'absolutely pure-brewed, entirely without sugar or chemicals' against the noise of the jazz band. Carling Black Label, with its 'Mabel' character, was first brewed in Britain in 1954. In the 1950s, lager actually constituted a tiny percentage of Britain's beer market and remained low until the 1970s.

The development of tourism encouraged advertising agencies to run campaigns linking their products with the delights of overseas travel. A 1959 advertisement for Booth's gin **ILLUSTRATION 82**, although appearing in an American magazine, shows the American tourist in Britain and the British tourist in America. Note in this colour painting the use of the stereotypical British and American images of a bobby and guardsman and a New York cop and skyscraper, making it an aspirational advertisement. You too could travel to such places if you drank Booth's gin. The same year Gordon's gin followed suit with a photographic advertisement showing a British Overseas Airways Corporation (BOAC) air hostess with her businessmen customers about to board their plane to fly to exotic destinations **ILLUSTRATION 83**.

The two main brandies, Martell and Hennessy, continued to advertise their products competitively to maintain their

ILLUSTRATION 83

The Illustrated London News, 1959

ILLUSTRATION 82

1959

Image courtesy of Diageo

Image courtesy of Diageo

Plus
ça
change,
plus
c'est
la même
chose*

1951   Royal Opera House, Covent Garden.   1900

🍾 HENNESSY 'X.O'
The Liqueur Cognac Brandy of **unvarying** Excellence

ILLUSTRATION 84

Country Life Annual, 1951

market share. A Hennessy advertisement appearing in the 1951 *Country Life Annual* is obviously aimed at the highest echelons of society **ILLUSTRATION 84** as its setting is the Royal Opera House in Covent Garden, London. Not only is the setting of the advertisement grand and exquisite, like the brandy, but the fashionable folk are accompanied by a French text. Five years later a Martell advertisement, in comparison, emphasises its Gallic heritage with a night-time French cityscape **ILLUSTRATION 85**.

A rival to Martini & Rossi in vermouth advertisements was another Italian company Cinzano, whose products became more popular in later decades. In a 1952 black and white advertisement **ILLUSTRATION 86**, Cinzano claims that 'all over the world more people drink Cinzano than any other vermouth' and associates London, flatteringly labelled the 'world's largest city', with the 'World's Largest Producers of Vermouth'. Hence the authority of Big Ben and Parliament symbolise the greatness of Cinzano.

ILLUSTRATION 85

The Illustrated London News, 1956

WORLD'S LARGEST CITY...

LONDON is the world's largest city covering an area of approx. 750 square miles, with over 17,000 streets aggregating many thousands of miles, and a population of over 8,000,000. In bars and hotels everywhere in London you will find prominently displayed CINZANO, the product of the World's Largest Producers of Vermouth.

Cinzano has an extra quality and a finer flavour than ordinary vermouths. That is why all over the world more people drink Cinzano than any other vermouth.

 Try it yourself—on its own or as a cocktail. You'll enjoy its delicious extra quality.

WORLD'S LARGEST
PRODUCERS OF VERMOUTH

RED (*Italian Sweet*)   WHITE (*Italian Sweet*) 17/- bottle, 9/- ½ bottle
DRY (*French*) 18/- bottle, 9/6 ½ bottle

Sole Importers: GIORDANO LTD., 24 CHARLOTTE STREET, LONDON, W.1 Tel. MUSeum 7274

ILLUSTRATION 86

Vogue, 1952

Where there's a
PIMM'S
there's a party

PIMM'S No.1 — THE MOST HEAVENLY DRINK ON EARTH

ILLUSTRATION 87

1954

The Englishman's* Guide t Smirnoff Vodka

The Island Race are among the world's most discerning drinkers. They are, however, notably conservative in their tastes, preferring to stick to what they know than experiment with alien beverages of doubtful potency. Believing, however, that Englishmen* should share in the pleasures of cocktail imbibers in other lands, we gladly provide a few facts about the world-famous Smirnoff Vodka.

1. Smirnoff Vodka is a smooth palatable drink, no stronger than your Gin, Whisky or Rum.

2. Smirnoff Vodka is today one of America's most popular drinks, where it is used as the blending spirit for new and established cocktails as well as for long drinks.

3. Smirnoff Vodka makes a most attractive drink taken straight "à la Russe," especially when accompanied by savouries.

4. Smirnoff Vodka is made in this country according to the traditional recipe used by Pierre Smirnoff, purveyor of Vodka to the Imperial Court of Russia.

Try Smirnoff instead of Gin in your favourite cocktail. Try a VODKATINI (Smirnoff Vodka and Vermouth mixed in your favourite proportions) and a SCREWDRIVER (Smirnoff Vodka and Orange Juice).

★ *To say nothing of the Scots, the Welsh and those of the Irish whose pleasure know no frontier.*

Smirnoff VODKA

THE GENUINE

WORLD FAMOUS SINCE 1818

OBTAINABLE FROM ALL GOOD WINE MERCHANTS, CLUBS AND BARS

Ste. Pierre Smirnoff Fls., Oval Road, Regents Park, London, N.W.1 • Sole distributors in U.K., W. & A. Gilbe

ILLUSTRATION 88

1954

Examples of advertising targeted at specific demographic groups include two advertisements from 1954. The first appeared in a Scottish magazine – hence the images of Scotsmen taking part in a variety of Highland Games events such as tossing the caber and playing the bagpipes **ILLUSTRATION 87**. Underneath, the unlikely message encourages them to drink Pimm's spirit drink at a party, rather than the more traditional whisky.

The second targeted advertisement is for Heublein, the American parent company of Smirnoff Russian vodka. In an attempt to sell its product in anti-communist America during this early Cold War period, Heublein spent a million dollars (a huge sum in its day) on its advertising campaign. To expand its market, the company opened its first British plant in the Fifties, which resulted in it becoming a brand leader until the arrival of Absolut

ILLUSTRATION 89

The Illustrated London News, 1956

vodka in the Eighties. This humorous black and white advertisement **ILLUSTRATION 88** targets the English, encouraging them to change from their home drinks of gin and whisky.

Mention must be made briefly of sherry and port, which were traditionally drunk before and after meals respectively. In a Dry Sack sherry advertisement **ILLUSTRATION 89**, a Spanish peasant and his donkey carry

"Look who's here!"

SANDEMAN
PORT

"You'll like it"

oversize bottles of sherry through the night, with a Surrealist-inspired shining sun symbolising the sunny nature of the product. A black and white cartoon for Sandeman port **ILLUSTRATION 90** contains the logo of the cloaked Sandeman offering port to four people watching television — an activity restricted to those few who could afford a set in 1952.

Having recovered from wartime shortages, whisky companies in the Fifties continued to run their traditional Christmas advertising campaigns. The Haig brand repeated its 1930s slogan 'Don't be vague ask for Haig' in a 1952 Christmas advertisement **ILLUSTRATION 91**. The scene is Christmas shopping in London's main streets and provides today's viewers with a picture of contemporary middle-class society through their fashions and the fact that all elements of society are represented — from men shopping alone to women, children and couples. It has the look of a Christmas card with the box at the bottom-right corner wishing viewers the season's compliments.

Don't be Vague
ask
for
Haig

With the Compliments
of the Season
JOHN HAIG & CO. LTD.

ILLUSTRATION 91

*The Illustrated London
News, 1952*

To friends everywhere we send hearty Christmas and New Year greetings and offer this crossword for amusement and relaxation.

'BLACK & WHITE'
SCOTCH WHISKY
The Secret is in the Blending

JAMES BUCHANAN & CO. LTD., Glasgow and London

ILLUSTRATION 92

The Illustrated London News, 1955

ING — and one by one men are
ng out the lights on their working day.
ght, quietly at home or gaily
d, they are once again husbands,
, friends among friends. Those who have
ed to savour each moment of their
re hours will crown contentment with a
(or two) of **Dewar's "White Label"**.

It never varies

ILLUSTRATION 93
1957

Everyone has a "double"—
when it's Vat 69!

ILLUSTRATION 94
The Illustrated London News, 1959

A Black & White blended Scotch whisky advertisement from three years later uses very similar imagery to promote its Christmas message **ILLUSTRATION 92**. The scene is post Christmas dinner when the people are enjoying a blazing fire, though the exact relationship of the men and women is not obvious. An added bonus of this advertisement is the inclusion of the actual crossword from the newspaper, for purchasers of the *Illustrated London News* to complete during the festive season.

Dewar's proud boast of being *the* whisky shows here a London scene at night stating clearly in the copy that it is socially acceptable for men to have a drink of Dewar's after the end of a day's work **ILLUSTRATION 93**.

The last three whisky advertisements in this chapter illustrate how varied the campaigns were. VAT 69 blended Scotch whisky, in a colourful, witty Christmas advertisement **ILLUSTRATION 94** contrasts the man in his

The friendly Scotch...

Long John WHISKY

**The proprietary Scotch Whisky
of world-wide renown**

DISTILLED, MATURED, BLENDED AND BOTTLED IN SCOTLAND

ILLUSTRATION 95

The Illustrated London News, 1959

dinner suit with a penguin, making literal use of a phrase often applied to such outfits. A month earlier in **ILLUSTRATION 95** for Long John whisky, the clichéd Scots scenery and the man in a bonnet with a glass of whisky in his hand emphasises the healthy properties of whisky (see **ILLUSTRATION 39**). Humour and tradition are replaced in Grant's advertisement by colourful, artistic, cubist-like images drawn by F.H.K. Henrion[4]

ILLUSTRATION 96. This was one of a series by Henrion which showed the influence of fine artists being involved in advertising, a trend which continued into the second half of the century.

4 F.H.K. Henrion (1914–1990) was born in Germany but adopted British nationality in 1946. During the 1950s he was art director at the Institute of Contemporary Arts (ICA). He often used elements of collage and photomontage in his work and was a pioneer of the use of Surrealist juxtapositions in advertising.

PUNCH OR THE LONDON CHARIVARI—MAY 27 1959

In the highlands, in the country places, where the old plain men have rosy faces,

and the young fair maidens, quiet eyes

ROBERT LOUIS STEVENSON

It is here in the highlands that Scotch Whisky was first distilled. A drink of many quiet and excellent qualities; at its best in GRANT'S STAND FAST in the tall triangular bottle.

ILLUSTRATION 96

Punch, 1959

Chapter 5

1960s

Lager and love

By the 1960s, seventy-five per cent of advertisements used colour photography, a trend which had begun in the Thirties. As technology made its use cheaper, photographic images became the norm instead of the painted or drawn artwork of previous decades. Two key components of consumer choice in the 1960s and throughout the century were availability and affordability of products, especially alcoholic drinks. The relative affluence of the Fifties continued into this decade as the population's growing disposable income and desire for consumer goods, holidays and drink encouraged companies and their advertisers to maximise their market shares. This was the era of London as the creative centre of British advertising. Although the advent of television advertising had made some impact on print advertising, with the increase in mass leisure time came the further development of specialist leisure magazines in many of which alcoholic drinks advertisements could be placed.

This was the decade when lager consumption began to have a greater impact. Before then, lager had been imported in expensive bottles and it was only when it began to be brewed under licence in Britain that young people and women became major consumers. Until then, mild beer had been the traditional male working-class drink. The 1961 Licensing Act allowed off-licence sales in shops and Sainsbury's was the first supermarket to sell alcohol. This in turn led to increased demand for bottles and cans for home consumption, especially in packs.

ILLUSTRATION 97

Punch, 1961

Make a party perfect —
e home **Long Life** in the new 6-pack
CANNED BEER

an IND COOPE product

Reproduced courtesy of Carlsberg UK Limited

ILLUSTRATION 98

The Illustrated London News, 1960

One of the first canned beers to be sold (in party packs) was Ind Coope's Long Life. An illustration from the period shows a couple sharing and enjoying a can of Long Life in a romantic setting under the stars ILLUSTRATION 97. A 1960 advertisement from the *Illustrated London News* announces the arrival of Skol lager, a new type of beer ILLUSTRATION 98. The advertisement targets men and women with the lengthy copy explaining why Skol should be drunk, including 'to meet today's tastes'. The name was chosen in keeping with the fashion

It's a refreshing world with **SKOL**

Say SKOL . . . and quench your thirst with this new International beer, now brewed to the same exacting standards all round the world. Say SKOL again and discover how clear and refreshing a really good beer can be. **Say SKOL – the International beer.**

Skol International is now in Holland-brewed by Verenigde Nederlandse Brouwerijen d'ORANJEBOOM, N.V.

ILLUSTRATION 99

1966

WHAT WE WANT **IS more WATNEYS**

More Watneys Pale Ale!

Watneys Pale . . . the nicest thing that ever happened to a thirst. It has a taste as fresh as a morn in Spring. It's a masterpiece of golden, glinting promise to look at—a mountain of pleasure to drink. And all yours for the asking!

AND TRY

WATNEYS BROWN ALE: more people drink it than any other brown ale . . .

WATNEYS HAMMERTON STOUT: brewed with oatmeal and glucose for zest . . .

WATNEYS DAIRYMAID STOUT: sweet, satisfying and inexpensive.

ILLUSTRATION 100

The New John Bull, 1960

of giving lagers continental names, in order to appeal to those people who could afford to go on cheap foreign holidays, where many first tasted European lagers. As if to emphasise this connection, a Skol international advertisement of 1966 shows a photograph of tourists and locals on a Caribbean beach **ILLUSTRATION 99**.

Watney's claimed in the early Sixties that its first draught keg beer, Red Barrel, was not only a premium product but also the country's favourite bitter. Sales of keg beer, which was most popular with young people, rose steadily

throughout the decade. Another Watney brand, Pale Ale, continued to appear in print advertisements (unlike Red Barrel) such as **ILLUSTRATION 100**, which associates the healthy, manly sport of sailing with the refreshing thirst-quenching taste of Pale Ale.

Whilst other brewing companies were competing with the arrival of lager, Benson's continued to produce its humorous original artwork advertisements for Guinness. Two examples from 1960 illustrate this point. The first is drawn by Gerard Hoffnung, an eccentric cartoonist of

5 MILLION GUINNESS
plus 92
for the orchestra

ARE ENJOYED EVERY DAY

ONCE YOU COME to appreciate Guinness it will be your friend for life. This is one of the world's *great* drinks. It isn't surprising that the world loves it.

More and more people are drinking Guinness. It would take you *weeks* to count the five million glasses enjoyed in *one* day. But why bother ! What you are interested in is your next Guinness and the strength and invigoration you find in it. So when it's Guinness Time, make straight for the nearest bar and join your friends in this popular drink. There's no Guinness like the next Guinness.

After work is Guinness Time. Enjoy your Guinness today

ILLUSTRATION 101
1960

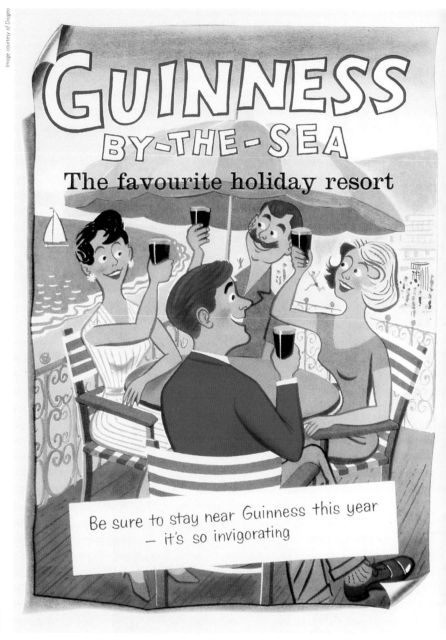

ILLUSTRATION 102
1960

musical instruments and musicians **ILLUSTRATION 101**. The copy states that five million glasses of Guinness were being drunk every day, and also reuses the Guinness gives 'strength' claim from the advertisements of the Thirties.

The second parodies the classic 'Skegness is bracing' poster by John Hassall[5] **ILLUSTRATION 102**.

5 John Hassall (1868–1948), illustrator of books and posters, especially famous for the 1908 'Skegness is so bracing' poster.

GOOD FOR YOU

"In my opinion after thirty-seven years of general medical practice, Guinness stands high in the help which it can give to many patients. I order it very frequently after such debilitating conditions as influenza and other toxic conditions which leave so many people flat and lacking in energy. I also think that Guinness is indicated towards the end of a day which, in these hectic times, is often filled with strain and worry." M.B., Ch.B.

The Doctor who wrote this letter has given us special permission to publish it.

Image courtesy of Diageo

ILLUSTRATION 103
1963

ILLUSTRATION 104
1969

I say "A Guinness a day keeps the doctor away"

It was Grandma's sixty-eighth birthday last Tuesday. She came over and spent the day with us, bursting with energy as usual. Goodness knows how she manages it!

Got a few extra Guinnesses in. She enjoys her daily Guinness just as much as I do. She believes it's what keeps her so fit and well.

On Friday nights it's Grandma who looks after the kids while Bill and I have a night out. It's usually the pictures, dancing or a slap-up meal. More often than not we meet up with friends at the local.

Fancy Bill taking a picture of me in this state! I laugh at it now, of course. But at the time it was hell; three weeks in hospital, and another three at home before they removed the plaster. Never again will I try jumping onto a moving bus, doesn't matter how much of a hurry I'm in!

GUINNESS is good for ~~you~~ me

Image courtesy of Diageo

Since the early 1940s Guinness's easily recognisable advertising style had been disappearing and so it was decided to revamp the Guinness image. The new lettering style developed by Bruce Hobbs appeared in a 1963 advertisement ILLUSTRATION 103. It harks back to the campaigns of the Thirties when Guinness beer was promoted as a health-giving product often supported by doctors' endorsements. Even at the end of the decade Guinness was still aiming its 'Good for you' advertisements at women claiming that a Guinness a day keeps the doctor away ILLUSTRATION 104. The mini-skirts and hairstyles fix it firmly in this period.

A rival to Guinness, Mackeson in this decade made up sixty per cent of Whitbread's sales. At the same time as Guinness was changing its image, Mackeson stout was being advertised in original and different ways. In a 1963 advertisement ILLUSTRATION 105 that appeared in *Country Life* magazine, curry and stout are colourfully presented together. The fashion was to drink water or beer with curry. It should be remembered that eating Indian food was a relatively recent development in Britain, as the immigration of the Fifties and Sixties led to the opening of Indian restaurants.

Happy meeting of east and west: curry and Mackeson

Perhaps you normally drink plain water with a curry. Or perhaps you drink plain beer. But why not try something original? Why not try a Mackeson? To those hot oriental flavours, Mackeson adds an urbane touch of the western world. It is cool and bland and mellow. Not sharp or heavy. A smooth and pleasing companion to the spices and peppers of the east. So next time you eat Indian, drink Mackeson. It turns the simplest curry into a feast fit for a maharajah.

ILLUSTRATION 105

Country Life, 1963

How to perform black magic

Burn your old formula for making Black Velvet, with suitable passes and incantations. Follow this new one instead :
1 pint champagne
1 bottle Mackeson
(both well cooled)

A transformation takes place. A somewhat heavy Edwardian drink disappears. In its place comes something much more to the taste of the moment : smoother, blander, free from bitterness. A Black Velvet, in fact, that for once lives up to its name. The hint of

sweetness in the Mackeson softens the edge of champagne. The fullness of the one blends happily with the sparkle of the other.
So, when you next want to exorcise low spirits, have a little dabble in the dark arts : make your Black Velvet with Mackeson.

ILLUSTRATION 106

The Illustrated London News, 1964

To demonstrate its flexibility, a Mackeson advertisement from the following year invited readers to perform Black Magic by mixing Mackeson stout and champagne to create the fashionable drink, black velvet

ILLUSTRATION 106. It was quite daring (though perhaps done with tongue in cheek) not only to refer to black magic but also to exorcising low spirits. The blackness of the advertisement reinforces the feeling of 'black' magic.

Tampering with your husband's Whitbread could be a little unwise.

Not only from his point of view, but from yours. Because, who knows?

That cool and sparkling Whitbread now disappearing down the plumbing could be the same cool and sparkling Whitbread you'll need in a day or two.

To soothe your palpitating husband over a sale, a bargain, or some other impetuous purchase.

("A Whitbread a day keeps the divorce lawyers at bay", old Whitbread proverb.)

So for the sake of your marriage, remember.

Our flavour is meant to go to his palate. Not to your head.

A word of caution to young wives.

Whitbread for choice

ILLUSTRATION 107

1969

To our friends at home and abroad
Greetings for a Happy Christmas
and a Good New Year

'BLACK & WHITE'
SCOTCH WHISKY
"BUCHANAN'S"

JAMES BUCHANAN & CO LTD · GLASGOW AND LONDON

ILLUSTRATION 108

The Illustrated London News, 1960

ILLUSTRATION 109
1963

Image courtesy of Diageo

Another innovative beer advertising campaign is illustrated in a 1969 Whitbread Pale Ale advertisement ILLUSTRATION 107. It shows the popular Sixties habit of women washing their hair in beer to give it extra shine. The copy appears very old-fashioned: the women are advised not to use the beer in this way as they may need to soothe their husbands 'over a sale, a bargain or some other impetuous purchase'. Here women are clearly portrayed as spending their husbands' money and not earning it themselves.

Whisky consumption in the Sixties also continued to increase. A witty Christmas 1960 advertisement for Black & White blended Scotch whisky ILLUSTRATION 108 shows Santa enjoying a glass of whisky, with a cigarette in hand, after delivering all the presents. This would no longer be permitted because of the government's restrictions, since the 1970s, on tobacco advertising.

A simple black and white advertisement for the VAT 69 brand ILLUSTRATION 109 invites the readers – who already go yachting, an expensive hobby even in the Sixties – to double their status by drinking this brand of whisky, which was still very much seen as a high-quality expensive product. Another brilliant advertisement of this period is for J&B blended Scotch whisky, which was at the time the second largest selling whisky after Cutty Sark ILLUSTRATION 110. The words pouring out of the bottle contain subtle references to the fact that whisky no longer had to be entirely exported to America.

Image courtesy of Diageo

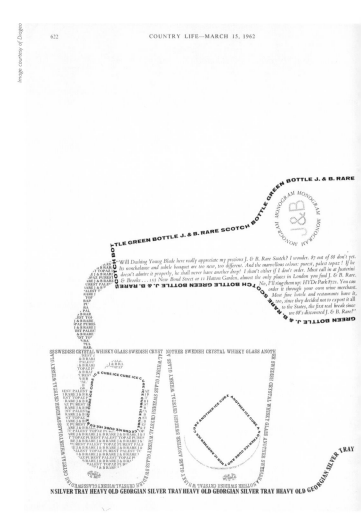

ILLUSTRATION 110
Country Life, 1962

In spite of our picture
a few masculine prerogatives remain;
and, until the rise of Cutty Sark,
whisky drinking was one of them.
No longer.
Women love this elegant Scotch because
it is lighter in colour, softer in touch...
It is indeed the man's Scotch
that women prefer.

The man's Scotch that women prefer

CUTTY SARK
SCOTCH WHISKY

ILLUSTRATION 111
Vogue, 1965

ILLUSTRATION 112
1966

Give color if you must

but the best entertainment
still comes in 'Black & White'

Dewar's
the scotch that speaks volumes

it never varies

ILLUSTRATION 113
Scottish Field, 1968

Women are targeted again in a 1965 *Vogue* advertisement for Cutty Sark **ILLUSTRATION 111** in which the cockpit, the domain of the male pilot, is occupied by a beautiful blonde drinking 'the man's Scotch that women prefer'.

A 1966 advertisement for Black & White blended Scotch whisky alludes to the arrival of colour television with a reference to the 'best entertainment' **ILLUSTRATION 112**. Dewar's employs double meaning in a 1968 advertisement drawn by Edward McLachlan.[6] The humour lies in the viewers knowing the tradition of secret doors hidden in bookcases of stately homes **ILLUSTRATION 113**.

6 Edward McLachlan (born 1940) is an illustrator and cartoonist whose work has appeared in magazines including *Punch*, *Private Eye*, newspapers, children's books and, of course, advertisements. http://www.edmclachlan.co.uk

IN TALL DRINKS
OR SHORT—
MIXED OR STRAIGHT—
Italy's most fashionable Aperitif
IS JUST
OUT OF THIS WORLD!

CAMPARI

YOU WILL LEARN TO LOVE IT!

ILLUSTRATION 114
1964

During the 1960s, a fashion developed for drinking aperitifs and liqueurs, either straight or mixed, especially amongst women. Traditionally such drinks were either consumed before or after meals rather than being drunk when out at social occasions. One such aperitif is Campari. A 1964 advertisement **ILLUSTRATION 114** links the first satellite to orbit the earth with its 'out of this world' product. Worth noting is the inclusion of the words 'you will learn to love it', deemed necessary because Campari has a bitter taste.

ILLUSTRATION 115

1964

ILLUSTRATION 116

1964

REMEMBER BEING PAINTED IN PARIS WITH A GLASS OF **DUBONNET**

Another liqueur with a bitter taste previously seen as having medicinal properties, Dubonnet, had become popular as a mixer drink, usually with lemonade ILLUSTRATION 115. The advertisement shows a couple on holiday in the exotic Montmartre district of Paris, drinking Dubonnet whilst an artist ostentatiously paints the bottle and not their portrait. European tourism as a theme appears in a Martini advertisement ILLUSTRATION 116 where a couple drink Martini whilst showing a friend their holiday slides. Note how, in both these advertisements, the more formal fashions of the couples compare with their holiday outfits and the artist's clothes.

The nights are drawing in, thank heaven. Darkness. And ice cubes. Coke. Or tonic. And Bacardi rum. Who needs sunshine? Just a bottle of Bacardi. But then it comes from the Bahamas. Hold your bottle up to the moon. Bacardi is pure, and clearer even than the Caribbean. This autumn, don't waste a single evening. Bacardi rum is the spirit of adventure.

The Bahamas are where the action is !

Bacardi and the Bat device are registered trade marks of Bacardi and Company Limited.

ILLUSTRATION 117
1966

A Bacardi rum advertisement consisting of photographs of actual places in the Caribbean ILLUSTRATION 117 exhorts the readers to drink Bacardi during the dark autumn days to remind them of their exotic summer holidays.[7] Bacardi enjoyed an annual growth rate of ten per cent during the Sixties as rum moved from being considered a lower-class drink to one drunk by those from the higher social classes who could afford to holiday in such places.

7 Cuba was not used as a location because of the Cuban missile crisis 1961–62. Russia had based some of its nuclear missiles on the island targeted at America.

ILLUSTRATION 118
1964

Cinzano used its Harlequin[8] figures in different ways in these two advertisements. Three leotard-wearing women represent the three different ways of drinking Cinzano Bianco ILLUSTRATION 118, whilst the Harlequin figure takes centre stage in an *Illustrated London News* advertisement ILLUSTRATION 119 stressing the mixability and social effect of the drink.

Drambuie, 'Scotland's pre-eminent contribution to the world's classic liqueurs' (Walton, 2006, p.453), was taking its place in the liqueur market at this time. A 1966 advertisement ILLUSTRATION 120 associates the product's sophistication with that of the then-current James Bond's movie, *Thunderball*, and its licence to thrill.

8 Harlequin was a comic character from the Italian commedia dell'arte (improvised drama) who was dressed usually in multicoloured diamond patterned costumes.

CINZANOSCOPE!

CINZANO
THE BIANCO

an exciting new taste, smooth, subtly sweet,
the unique full strength white vermouth.

short with lemon peel | long with soda and ice | mixed with gin or vodka

CINZANO DRY FRENCH ◆ CINZANO RED

HAVEN'T TRIED SMIRNOFF? WHERE IN THE WORLD HAVE YOU BEEN?

You must have been on another planet if you haven't tried one of these delicious Smirnoff drinks: Smirnoff and orange juice. Smirnoff and tomato juice. Smirnoff and 7-Up®—the new Smirnoff Mule. Only smooth, flawless Smirnoff makes so *many* drinks so well! For only Smirnoff is filtered through 14,000 pounds of activated charcoal to blend perfectly with anything that pours. Nothing less will do for your party. Smirnoff shows you *know*. Smirnoff says you *care*.

Always ask for *Smirnoff* It leaves you breathless® VODKA

men
make
passes
at **PIMMS**
in
glasses...

girls love PIMMS,

Image courtesy of Diageo

ILLUSTRATION 121

McCall's Magazine, 1965

ILLUSTRATION 122

The Illustrated London News, 1964

Like the Campari advertisement of a year earlier, Smirnoff's message was that its vodka was literally out of this world, linking the increasingly competitive space race between Russia and America with a female astronaut and

Russian vodka **ILLUSTRATION 121**. Both vodka and rum were beginning to make serious inroads into the whisky market. An old saying is used to great humorous effect here in a summer 1964 advertisement for the Pimm's

AT CHRISTMAS-TIME EVERYONE SAYS—
I'D LOVE A BABYCHAM

WHEN WE'RE ALL TOGETHER
WE'LL NEED LOTS OF BABYCHAM

Image courtesy of Diageo

ILLUSTRATION 123
1961

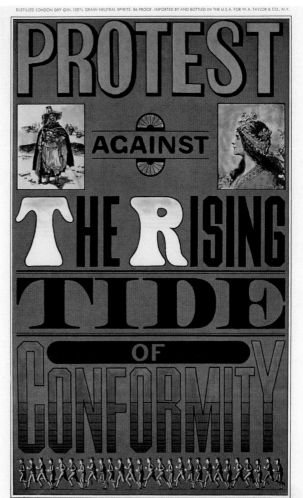

DISTILLED LONDON DRY GIN. 100% GRAIN NEUTRAL SPIRITS. 86 PROOF. IMPORTED BY AND BOTTLED IN THE U.S.A. FOR W.A. TAYLOR & CO., N.Y.

PROTEST AGAINST THE RISING TIDE OF CONFORMITY

Serve Booth's House of Lords, the non-conformist gin from England.

Then declare yourself. Get a laminated copy of our poster's message. Ready to frame, hang or stand. Send request (and one dollar to cover the usual) to "Protest," Dept. A, P.O. Box 74, Lindenhurst, New York. Offer good only where legal.

ILLUSTRATION 124
1965

brand ILLUSTRATION 122 showing the tall 'male' glasses and the rounder shorter 'female' glasses echoing differences in men's and women's body shapes.

Just as whisky companies ran extensive campaigns in the run up to Christmas, so too did other companies such as Babycham ILLUSTRATION 123, in this case boasting that it is the 'happiest drink in the world'. The six pack here echoes the packs of beer advertised in this decade as being a necessity for any good party.

The 'Swinging Sixties', as a time when young people were challenging the accepted social norms, is perfectly captured in two gin advertisements. In the first, the Booth's brand's usual image as a very traditional, socially upright drink of the upper classes is inverted ILLUSTRATION 124. Its imagery could also be interpreted as a commentary on the protests against racism taking place in America at that time. In the second, for Gordon's

1769: Gordon's Gin

The fad was more "Fop" than "Mod" when Londoner Alexander Gordon developed his fabulous gin recipe. But the thing for gin to be then was the same thing gin should be now. Dry! Gordon's is so dry it's known as the "martini gin" to many a pernickety martini-ite. Biggest seller in England, America, the world.

1968: Gordon's 'Cranaby St.'

Psychedelic in color. Light, sassy, delicious in taste. A tall, lanky drink that's tart and tingling. Start with a tall, slim glass. Add ice and the juice of ½ a lemon. Pour in 1½ oz. of Glorious Gordon's Gin and 3 oz. of cranberry juice. Add two drops of bitters and a splash of soda water. Stir.

What will the English think of next?

PRODUCT OF U.S.A. 100% NEUTRAL SPIRITS DISTILLED FROM GRAIN. 90 PROOF. GORDON'S DRY GIN CO., LTD., LINDEN, N.J.

ILLUSTRATION 125

1968

Image courtesy of Diageo

gin **ILLUSTRATION 125**, the advertisement's background uses Sixties psychedelic colours combined with a sign, clearly referring to Carnaby Street, the centre of the Sixties fashion scene. The advertisement was probably aimed at the American tourist market.

Mention must be made here of the scarcity of advertisements for wine. This was because wine was relatively expensive and traditionally considered the preserve of the wealthier members of society. Towards the end of the Sixties, this image changed – in part due to mass production and importation, mainly of French and German wines; the influence of European package holidays; and changes in tastes and fashions. Having tasted wine whilst on holiday, Britons started to drink wine with meals both at home and in restaurants. An early example of this trend was the popularity of Mateus Rosé wine **ILLUSTRATION 126**, which in the Seventies was to become a classic cheap drink for students, many of whom made the bottles (along with Chianti ones) into lamps!

Before concluding this chapter, reference needs to be made to the government's anti-drink driving campaigns, which began in the Forties. Despite these, there had been a steady increase in fatalities caused by drunken drivers; so with the introduction of the breathalyser in October 1967, the government launched one of its regular campaigns emphasising what a huge amount could be lost if a person were convicted of drink driving **ILLUSTRATION 127**.

The 17th Century Palace of Mateus, Douro, Northern Portugal   Photograph by Percy Hennell

MATEUS ROSÉ

the enchanting pink wine

ILLUSTRATION 126

1960s

Don't ask a man to drink and <u>drive</u> –

he's got too much to lose

You <u>know</u> it makes sense

ILLUSTRATION 127

1960s

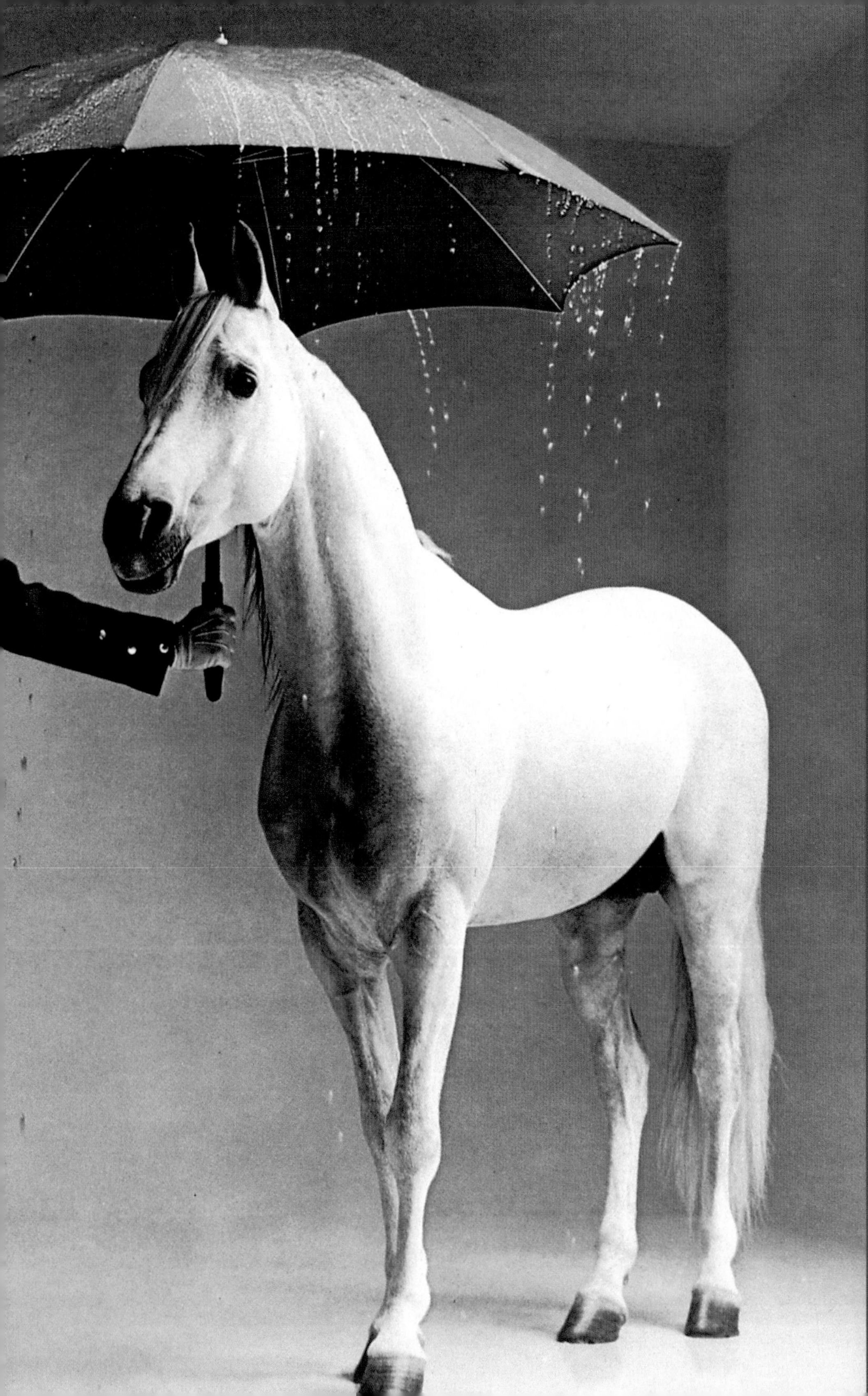

Chapter 6

1970s

Anything goes

The 1970s is considered by some to have been another golden age of British advertising, when several iconic alcoholic drinks campaigns were launched. In a 2002 interview, Tim Mellors considered Guinness 'to be one of the consistently greatest campaigns of the second half of the twentieth century' (Mellors, 2002, p.50). In 1969 Guinness had changed to J. Walter Thompson (JWT), only its second advertising agency in forty years as it was felt that the product should appeal to a wider audience. This agency attempted to increase Guinness's sales through refreshing the humour of the previous campaigns and targeting women drinkers; it also tried to 'place Guinness squarely in the beer market, reinforce its uniqueness and begin challenging some of the prejudices that existed about Guinness' (Sibley, 1985, p.160). In a 1971 advertisement **ILLUSTRATION 128**, JWT uses advertising buzzwords with a large amount of text to remind Guinness drinkers, and tell others, about the benefits of Guinness. Its poster campaigns parodied contemporary blockbuster films: where *A Fistful of Dollars* starred Clint Eastwood, 'A Fistful of Guinness' allegedly featured a 'tall, dark and have some draught'.

The targeting of women was partly in response to the growth of feminism and the women's liberation movement. As they joined the workforce in even greater numbers, a large market of financially independent women developed. Ann Leworthy, JWT's Art Director, conceived a provocative campaign using the image of a

After two centuries of drinking Guinness regularly (purely in the interests of science) we have found that the following method is the most reliable: raise the glass to your lips, tilt it gently towards you (tilting it away from you is not nearly so effective) and take a hearty swig. Make sure you drink the black part through the white part (in fact, it's difficult to do it the other way round) and then you can enjoy that unique mingling of the light smooth head and the dry, dark body. A strong, very civilized taste, you might think. Before you reach this stage, however, there are a number of other questions you may have to ask yourself, such as . . .

A. Head. Brewed by head brewer

Insert hand here.

B. Under. Brewed by under brewer

Drink B. through A.

HOW?

How do you pour a bottle of Guinness? How do you get that fine beer out of the bottle and into the glass?
Method 1: Remove bottle cap, grasp bottle firmly in right hand and pour beer slowly into a glass held at 47° to the perpendicular. Make sure that you pour it over the point where your thumb touches the glass as this helps the formation of the head. Slowly raise glass to upright position.
Method 2: Get the barmaid to pour it for you. The second method, you will observe, is much easier than the first and provided that the barmaid uses the first method, the results are exactly the same.

WITH?

We don't altogether approve of mixing Guinness with other drinks. The only thing you can probably add to a bottle of Guinness to improve it is another bottle of Guinness. (That makes it exactly twice as good.) But we must confess that if you can't find any neat Guinness, then Black Velvet (Guinness and Champagne, fifty-fifty) is an acceptable substitute. You make it in a jug and serve it on Sunday mornings to hordes of thirsty (grateful) friends. With any luck, they'll invite you back next week. But when we hear of people mixing it with tonic water or orange juice and even, in extreme cases, with ginger ale, we can't help feeling that it's a sad waste of a beautiful beer.

COOLED GUINNESS

WHICH?

There are two kinds of Guinness: Draught and Bottled. Draught Guinness comes in casks and is usually served in pints. Bottled Guinness is more often drunk in glasses, which makes it an ideal beer when your house is on fire and you've only time for a quick one.

Draught Guinness has a denser, whiter head and is served at a cooler temperature than Bottled Guinness as a rule. Bottled Guinness, however, spends at least three weeks maturing inside the bottle, which some people think accounts for that extra touch of dryness. (Well, how would you feel if you'd been kept in a bottle for three weeks?)

WHERE?

There are about 78,000 pubs in Britain and, as far as we know, all of them sell Bottled Guinness. Draught Guinness, on the other hand, is only sold in every other pub. You can also drink Guinness in licensed clubs, on trains, aircraft and pleasure steamers (if they don't serve Guinness they're just called ordinary steamers). And you can buy non-returnable bottles of our beer in off-licences and most licensed supermarkets, which means that you can enjoy them anywhere from the upper reaches of the Amazon (see illustration) to the security of your own home. Drinking Guinness at home is rather different from drinking Guinness in a pub (unless, of course, you happen to live in a pub) because you don't have to worry about closing time. In fact you can have the best of both worlds by making sure that whenever the man says "Last orders, please . . ." you pick up a few bottles to take home.

WHY?

Occasionally, when you are standing in a pub, quietly drinking our beer, some buffoon of less discriminating tastes may approach you and ask, "Why are you drinking Guinness?" You may then say:

1 I'm thirsty.
2 My mother-in-law's just moved in.
3 My mother-in-law's just moved out.
4 I can afford to drink the best beer in the pub.
5 I've just been made managing director of my firm.
6 Mind your own business.
7 It's my birthday.
8 It's not my birthday.
9 It was somebody else's round.
10 It was somebody else's pint.
11 I'm very choosy about the beer I drink.
12 I've just been made King.
13 The pub ran out of everything else.
14 It's groovy, man.
15 I have been persuaded by their cunning advertising.
16 I like the taste.
17 I own the brewery.
18 That's funny, I ordered a large scotch.

How to drink Guinness

ILLUSTRATION 128

Punch, 1971

Image courtesy of Diageo

GUINNESS

EVENING LENGTH BLACK DRINK

The trouble with most shorts is that they're just too short.
You spend too little time drinking them and too long wondering where the next one's coming from.
Tonight, slip into a long, flowing creation from the House of Guinness.
It's smooth, dark and in perfect taste. And it lasts a good deal longer than the drinks you're used to.
Guinness. You could find it suits you right down to the ground.

ILLUSTRATION 129
Vogue Food, 1976

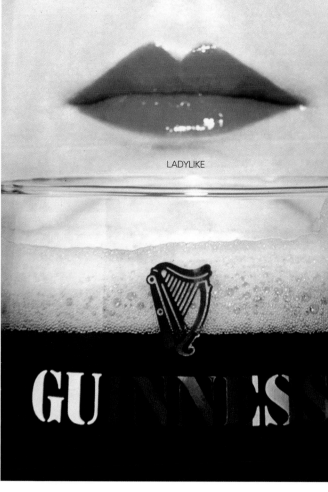

Image courtesy of Diageo

LADYLIKE

GU NNES

ILLUSTRATION 130
1974

woman's little black dress, alluding to a sophisticated, glamorous, sexy image of Seventies woman. One example is **ILLUSTRATION 129** with its copy, 'evening length black drink'.

The use of fashion photography was a trend that developed in this decade. This can be seen in an advertisement from the Guinness 'black goes with everything' campaign, which shows seven fashionably

dressed women, the copy implying that black surpasses all fashion trends. A 1977 advertisement shows a woman with cropped hair wearing a little black backless dress, holding a glass of Guinness beer and looking provocatively at the viewer. The copy claimed that women drink Guinness because 'they like its strong distinctive taste'. Women could now be thought as strong as men and so would enjoy Guinness, traditionally a masculine drink. Nevertheless, the last line – 'but we have

Heineken. Refreshes the parts other beers cannot reach.

ILLUSTRATION 131
Punch, 1976

to admit that a pretty girl with a Guinness still stands out from the crowd just a bit!' – reduces it to the level of sexual success.

A Guinness advertisement where sex was blatantly used to sell the product can be seen in **ILLUSTRATION 130**. Although these campaigns did not result in large numbers of women becoming regular Guinness drinkers, they were nevertheless a popular series of advertisements – especially with men.

Beer consumption rose throughout this decade. Lager had become very popular as high-priced imported bottles were replaced by draught lager brewed under licence in Britain and sales from supermarkets grew. One of the iconic lager advertising slogans from this decade belongs to Heineken, whose 'Refreshes the parts other

beers cannot reach' was coined by Terry Lovelock of the Collet Dickinson Pearce (CDP) agency in 1975. Although completely nonsensical, Lovelock 'created an oblique but powerful property for Heineken that defied both research and the reality of Heineken's lack of differentiation from other lagers' (Mellors, 2002, p.47). A whole series of these humorous advertisements was produced **ILLUSTRATION 131**. Some referred to contemporary films or television programmes such as *Star Trek* – in one advertisement, Doctor Spock's droopy ears stand up after he drinks Heineken. Unlike the Guinness advertisements of the same period, these advertisements did not suggest that Heineken could make you more socially popular, only that it could make you feel better in yourself. Here the slogan became synonymous with the product.

What happens when a Cockney Trophy Bitter drinker tries Liverpool's local Trophy?

Harry tumbles his first big loaf north of Watford and gets a grand-father clock.

Translation:
(Harry samples his first pint of Whitbread 'Bighead' Trophy Bitter outside London and gets something of a shock.)
"Apple fritter always 'as been me favourite tumble, know wot I mean? A nice 'ackney marsh o' Whitbread Big Loaf's my idea of 'eaven."
(Bitter always has been my favourite tipple, actually. There's nothing I like better than a glass of Whitbread 'Bighead' Trophy.)
"Well, I was up near the Pool last week in me old annie, fancied a swift Loaf, stopped at the first Whitbread rub-a-dub and got the grandfather of me life."
(Near Liverpool last week in my lorry, I felt like a 'Bighead,' stopped at a Whitbread public house and got a real shock.)

"Liverpool Loaf's nuffin like it is down the local battle cruiser!"
(I discovered that the taste of Trophy in Liverpool varies slightly from the taste of Trophy in my own local.)
"The barman told me Whitbread make sure the taste of the Loaf varies to understand the local bung, see."
(This, the barman explained, is because Whitbread brew Trophy to understand the local tongue, as it were, to suit local tastes.)
"Still, even though the taste may hail-mary from place to place, the quality certainly stays in the game."
(Still, even though the taste may vary from place to place, the quality certainly stays the same.)
"Down the Coiney!"
(Jolly good health to you!)

Whitbread 'Bighead' Trophy Bitter. Brewed to understand the local tongue.

Trophy is brewed by local Whitbread breweries in Blackburn, Cardiff, Castle Eden, Cheltenham, Faversham, Kirkstall, Liverpool, Luton, Marlow, Portsmouth, Rhymney, Romsey, Salford, Samlesbury, Sheffield, and Tiverton.

ILLUSTRATION 132

Punch, 1976

ILLUSTRATION 133

1972

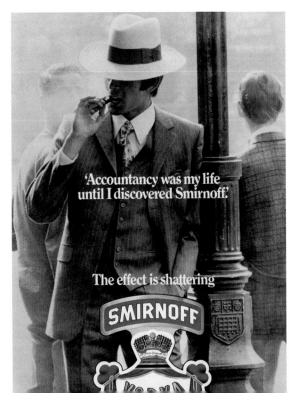

'Accountancy was my life until I discovered Smirnoff.'

The effect is shattering

SMIRNOFF

Humour was also used to great effect by a rival beer company Whitbread, which had breweries all over the country, in a series of advertisements. **ILLUSTRATION 132** uses cockney language to entice southern drinkers to try Trophy Bitter which was actually brewed in the north.

Before moving on to the advertising of spirits in the 1970s, mention must be made of the Campaign for Real Ale (CAMRA). Founded in 1971 in an era of large breweries selling keg beer, its aim was to return to cask-brewed beers. By the late Seventies, CAMRA had been very successful in that many of these companies had brought real ale back to their pubs. Despite taking on these companies, CAMRA used its funds not to advertise but on its campaigns and publications such as the *Good Beer Guide*.

Vodka had become a major player in the spirits market since the Sixties as drinkers became more familiar with its taste. It was consumed by all social classes, but especially by the 18 to 24 age group. Heublein spent one-tenth of its sales on advertising during this period. The advertisements were sophisticatedly humorous and far removed from traditional spirit advertising through the use of fantastic illusions. The first campaign refers to professionals having their lives brightened up by drinking Smirnoff **ILLUSTRATION 133**. In this example, the grey accountant is enlivened by the earth-shattering Smirnoff taste.

The second campaign of the late 1970s uses equally implausible scenarios to promote Smirnoff, implying that

ILLUSTRATION 134

1977

ILLUSTRATION 135

Photoplay, 1974

you'll experience life-changing events when you drink it. The slogan 'Well, they said anything could happen' **ILLUSTRATION 134** here applies to a fruit machine dispensing its jackpot as real fruit. As in the previous advertisement, only the top of the bottle label is shown. In another example, deliberately contrived to make viewers do a double take, a woman dressed in diving gear and flippers, holding a glass of Smirnoff, is falling to earth without a parachute beside a professional parachutist. It is worth noting the early reference in this advertisement to responsible drinking – 'remember whatever happens,

don't overdo it' – the promotion of which was developed more fully in the 1980s.

Whilst Smirnoff was running its humorous advertising campaigns, some of the other spirit companies were sticking to more traditional advertising techniques of using only the brand and its attributes. Promoted as an essential mixer for parties, Bacardi is shown in a 1974 advertisement **ILLUSTRATION 135** as if it were part of a school scientific experiment using tonic water. With a clever reference back to the long hot summer of 1976,

ILLUSTRATION 136

1978

We're in for a Dry spell.

Hot, blazing sun. Electric blue sky. Warm sand. Long,
lazy afternoons.
If it weren't for the cool, refreshing taste that springs
from Martini Dry's unique blend of fine wines and herbs...
Well, the whole thing would be just too much to bear.

MARTINI Extra Dry. The right one. Just by itself.

a Martini advertisement **ILLUSTRATION 136** radiates the
heat of the beach, where 'the right one' quenches thirst.
A third advertisement containing only the product
employs the device of wordplay to promote Campari's
uniqueness and ultimate pleasure **ILLUSTRATION 137**. As
advertisers might say: 'Don't sell the steak, sell the sizzle'
(Pollay, 1985, p.25).

Other kinds of connections were made in a 1973
Hennessy brandy advertisement. It compares the effect
that wearing an expensive Vionnet dress or a skimpy bikini
has on others with those of drinking a glass of Hennessy
– and in doing so, makes its own attempt to get its readers'
hearts racing **ILLUSTRATION 138**. An early example of a
humorous Grand Marnier campaign is seen in a 1971
advertisement by TBWA (an amalgamation of four
different agencies and long-time advertising agency for
Carillon, Grand Metropolitan Group) **ILLUSTRATION 139**.

The contents of whisky advertisements in the Seventies
appear to be a mixture of social commentary, products
and their attributes, and outrageous name associations. All
are concerned with swimming through the whisky loch
and overcoming the effects of a glut in unsold product,
caused by a slump in sales of whisky to America, whose
own brand whiskeys had grown and regained their
profits. A tongue in cheek 1971 advertisement for
Ballantine's was aimed at the liberated women's market,
a target for many drinks companies at this time. Three
fashionably dressed women stand at a bar drinking

There comes a time in life when you've tried everything, done it all. Or so you think. That's the time you should track down Campari, Italy's definitive aperitif. Pour out a generous measure, add chunks of ice, a slice of orange and top it up with a shoosh of soda. Then, very slowly and deliberately, empty the glass. Within seconds you'll realise that there's really…

No Camparison.

ILLUSTRATION 137

1972

ILLUSTRATION 138

Country Life, 1993

The French have always known how to make your heart beat a little faster.

Le Bikini 1954…….!

Vionnet 1921 – one of the first great French haute couture designers – she created for all the fashionable ladies of the decade.

Hennessy Cognac. First started hearts beating a little faster in 1765.

ILLUSTRATION 139

Gourmet, 1971

Past
Historic
1884

Present
Indicative
1979

The **Buchanan** Blend
THE SCOTCH OF A LIFETIME

ILLUSTRATION 140
1979

One colour always unites the clans.

Black is the ultimate in whisky.

ILLUSTRATION 141
Time, 1979

whisky, whilst each thinks her 'liberated' thoughts – for example 'liberty, equality and Ballantine', a take on the slogan of the French Revolution. This blatantly associated the liberation of women to drink whisky with the massive social and political changes of that period in French history.

More traditional male whisky drinkers, who still accounted for the largest percentage of the whisky sales

market, were the target of a 1979 Buchanan's blended Scotch whisky advertisement **ILLUSTRATION 140**. The whisky is shown here as a luxurious Christmas present, whose consistent high-quality is intimated by the equal prominence given to the 1884 and 1979 bottles. The wordplay consolidates this link of past to present by associating them with an understanding of complex grammatical tenses, thus also implying that this brand is the intelligent choice.

ILLUSTRATION 142

Punch, 1977

water it down, pour it on ice, ginger it up, take it long, or neat, soda splashed or with lemon...

BELL'S
Scotland's Number One Scotch

Image courtesy of Diageo

The Johnnie Walker brand was particularly badly hit by the 'whisky loch' due to eighty-five per cent of its sales being for export. Here, using the somewhat clichéd imagery of Scottish tartans, the company associates its Black Label brand with uniting the clans which had feuded for centuries **ILLUSTRATION 141**. Could it be interpreted, perhaps, as a way of bringing people back together during the 1979 British 'Winter of Discontent'?[9] Although purist whisky drinkers would have been offended by a Bell's blended Scotch whisky advertisement **ILLUSTRATION 142**, it was targeting the wider market of those who added other beverages to their neat whisky.

One of the most famous whisky advertising campaigns of this decade is for White Horse blended Scotch whisky. The London-based advertising agency Langley Kingley Manton Palmer employed the photographer Michael Joseph to photograph a real white horse in various settings. Just as the black and white terriers are associated with Black & White blended Scotch whisky, the association of an animal with this product reinforces the brand's name by a visual pun **ILLUSTRATION 143**. Twenty-three of these advertisements were shot over the years. In a later

ILLUSTRATION 143

1971

You can take a White Horse anywhere

Image courtesy of Diageo

9 The large stoppage of work by thousands of British workers in the winter of 1978–9, caused by the Labour Government's attempt to enforce limits on pay rises in order to curb inflation.

ILLUSTRATION 145

1972

SCOTCH AND WATER.

ILLUSTRATION 144

Punch, 1978

example **ILLUSTRATION 144**, the white horse symbolises the whisky whilst the rain symbolises the water.

Babycham also continued to successfully promote itself to young women drinkers, as in this colour advertisement of 1972 **ILLUSTRATION 145** in which party time and Babycham are inextricably linked. Another specialist product, Pimm's spirit drink, used a couple at a party wearing 1920s costumes as a parodic reference to the film *The Godfather* **ILLUSTRATION 146**. In contrast to this, a 1974 Pernod advertisement **ILLUSTRATION 147** shows the bottle, drinks and their recipes, all distributed around an exquisitely drawn couple in a Sixties version of art nouveau.

Image courtesy of Diageo

There is nothing like a Pimm's
at a time like this.

Nothing so cool, so spirited or so special. Yet so simple to make.
At memorable moments like this, there's no drink in the world quite like a Pimm's.

PIMM'S

IT TAKES TWO TO "PERNOD"

Pernod...the versatile aperitif
Pernod is a drink with a bright new taste. The intriguing taste of anise. It's so refreshing you'll enjoy it anytime—before lunch, during brunch, at the cocktail hour, or the whole night through. Share it with anyone who likes a friendly new taste.

Pernod and Water
Pour 1½ oz. Pernod over ice cubes in tall glass. Fill with water.

Piña Pernod
Pour 1½ oz. Pernod over ice cubes in tall glass. Fill with pineapple juice.

Pernod and Orange Juice
Pour 1½ oz. Pernod over ice cubes in old-fashioned glass. Fill with orange juice.

Tomate
Pour 1½ oz. Pernod over ice cubes in tall glass. Add a dash of Grenadine. Fill with water and stir.

Sparkling Pernod
Pernod is delightful with Bitter Lemon or club soda and a slice of lemon.

PERNOD®
A New Taste

90 Proof

GOURMET/NOVEMBER 1974

ILLUSTRATION 147

Gourmet, 1974

ILLUSTRATION 146

Vogue, 1974

1970s ANYTHING GOES   **117**

ILLUSTRATION 148

Punch, 1971

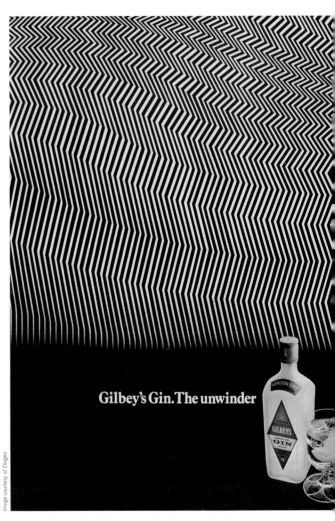

ILLUSTRATION 149

Vogue, 1973

GORDON'S DRY GIN

It's got to be Gordon's

Image courtesy of Diageo

ILLUSTRATION 150

1976

The major gin companies produced very different advertising campaigns from one another during this decade, although all with the same aim of growing their brand loyalty. Booth's photographed a young couple dressed in fashionable orange outfits to attract the younger market by suggesting that drinking Booth's gin and orange juice could make you more socially and sexually attractive **ILLUSTRATION 148**. A Gilbey's gin advertisement of a few years later uses only a photograph of the bottle and a glass on a Bridget Riley[10]

style background to sell the product to those wishing to de-stress **ILLUSTRATION 149**. The last of these three gin advertising campaigns is for the Gordon's brand. Its iconic green bottle advertisements appeared in the press, the cinema and on television **ILLUSTRATION 150**. The product's name and bubbles were sufficient to whet the appetite for a thirst-quenching Gordon's gin.

10 Bridget Riley (born 1931), proponent of op art and famous for her black and white geometric forms.

"A bottle of Blue Nun
and the menu."

Blue Nun from SICHEL
right through the meal.

ILLUSTRATION 151
1976

In the Seventies, wine consumption continued to grow. This was due to greater availability from supermarkets, the reduction of duty on wine (and hence its price) through European Community ruling, and advertising campaigns appearing in women's magazines as more women drank lighter wines such as Mateus Rosé and the sweeter German Blue Nun **ILLUSTRATION 151**. This major change in social habits is referred to by Burnett as 'the democratization of wine-drinking being a symbol of this change for people who before the war would not have contemplated wine with a meal' (Burnett, 1999, p.155).

The government's anti-drink driving campaign was continued into the 1970s with an advertisement **ILLUSTRATION 152** created by the Wasey Campbell-Ewald agency which altered a well-known sea shanty to 'What do we do with the drunken driver?' In graphic terms, the content shows what would happen if you were convicted of drink-driving offences. At the same time the Health Education Council was highlighting the dangers to men's sexual health of binge-drinking as this 1978 example shows **ILLUSTRATION 153**. It wittily adapts the Heineken slogan to state that beer drunk to excess has the opposite effect to that claimed by Heineken!

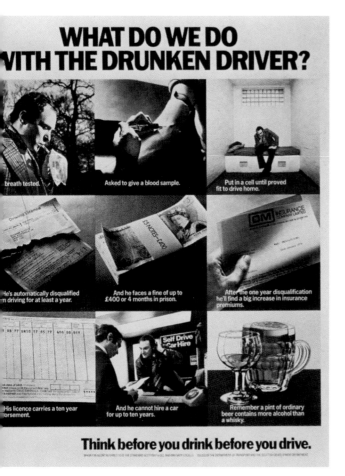

ILLUSTRATION 152

1979

If you drink too much there's one part that every beer can reach.

Your health isn't the only thing which suffers if you over-drink. A night of heavy drinking can make it impossible for you to make love.

And even if you think your drinking isn't affecting you, have you ever wondered how it might be affecting your partner?

Put it this way. How would you like to be made love to by a drunk?

The Health Education Council. Everybody likes a drink. Nobody likes a drunk.

ILLUSTRATION 153

1978

Chapter 7

1980s

Absolute perfection

During the 1980s beer consumption decreased, due partly to large price rises and partly to the economic recession of a Britain dominated by Thatcherism. Another reason was that public houses were under threat of being converted by the breweries into restaurants. Lager, which by this time made up more than forty per cent of the beer market, was being even more heavily promoted by many companies as they strove to differentiate their very similar brands. Carlsberg's 1970s slogan 'probably the best lager in the world' has been altered in this advertisement ILLUSTRATION 154 to 'probably the best *beer* in the world' in order to appeal to a wider market. Once again, an advertisement uses images of space exploration, in this case linking Carlsberg to the recent launch of the American space shuttle, to imply that the taste of its beer is out of this world.

Heineken continued its successful 'refreshes the parts' campaign as illustrated in this surreal advertisement ILLUSTRATION 155. At the same time, it began promoting itself as an international high-quality fashionable beer,

ILLUSTRATION 154

Time, 1985

ILLUSTRATION 155

1980s

Heineken refreshes the parts other beers cannot reach.

This is the kind of testimonial
we like best.

When you make a great beer, you don't have to make a great fuss.

ILLUSTRATION 156

1989

something so good that little advertising copy or imagery was required to get its message across ILLUSTRATION 156. The Heineken 'Beyond reach' campaign was very cheekily parodied by the Saatchi and Saatchi advertising agency as part of its campaign for Castlemaine XXXX, an Australian lager first brewed in 1878. It shows Sir Les Paterson (a fictional Australian character portrayed by comedian Barry Humphries) drinking a glass of Heineken that has absolutely no effect on him ILLUSTRATION 157.

ILLUSTRATION 157

1989

Beyond reach.

BECAUSE AUSTRALIANS WOULDN'T GIVE
A XXXX FOR ANYTHING ELSE.

You could probably do with a Guinness tonight.

ILLUSTRATION 158
1981

The Guinness brand's toucan was revived in 1979 by the JWT agency as a means of celebrating fifty years of Guinness advertising. This humorous advertisement ILLUSTRATION 158 appeared in the press timed to coincide with the showing of Steven Spielberg's film *Jaws* on British television, the message being that drinking Guinness gives you courage. Nevertheless, despite campaigns that were successful in so far as they encouraged non-Guinness drinkers to try the brand, sales continued to drop as consumers' affection for the toucan started to detract from the actual product.

ILLUSTRATION 159

1982

This prompted a change of advertising agencies. Allen Brady Marsh took over the Guinness account in 1982 with the main objective of promoting Guinness beer, by now a global brand, to the younger male sector of the British population, which made up over seventy per cent of all beer drinkers. Its 'Guinnless isn't good for you' ILLUSTRATION 159 campaign cost seven million pounds and was initially successful in achieving a phenomenal eighty-seven per cent spontaneous recall among British adults (Davies, 1998, p.155). This resulted in a revitalisation of Guinness's position in the beer market especially amongst younger drinkers. Nonetheless, its 'negative' slogan ultimately caused offence to the Guinness Company, which prided itself on the quality of its product. So, two years later another agency, Ogilvy & Mather, launched its 'Pure Genius' campaign ILLUSTRATION 160. This could refer to the drink or the drinkers, the two main aims being to put across the message that Guinness was 'mysterious, elemental, nourishing, rewarding and relaxing' and to appeal to the Guinness drinker 'masculine,

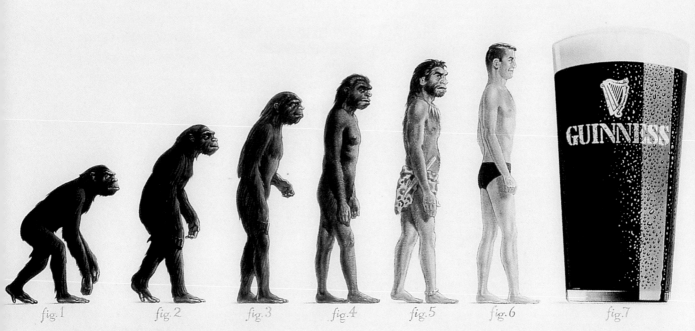

GUINNESS. PURE GENIUS.

ILLUSTRATION 160

1984

ILLUSTRATION 161

1981

Image courtesy of Diageo

individual, independent and in control' (Davies, 1998, p.162). All these values made references to the long history of Guinness advertising.

Twenty-eight years after the Queen's coronation had been celebrated by whisky companies, the royal wedding of her son H.R.H. Prince Charles (heir to the British throne) to Lady Diana Spencer in 1981 was a huge national celebration marked by a public holiday. Bell's blended Scotch whisky commemorated this event, which had worldwide press coverage, through its issue of a special whisky bottle ILLUSTRATION 161.

ILLUSTRATION 162

Telegraph Sunday Magazine, 1980

Some of the whisky companies during the Eighties also started targeting the younger market, whose preference was still for vodka, as a means of revitalising their market shares. J&B produced a series of visually humorous and abstract advertisements, in which the emphasis was no longer on the taste of the product ILLUSTRATION 162. Chivas Regal, which had previously had a large number of different advertising campaigns over the years, was also targeting this sector. In a 1983 advertisement, Chivas Regal is the priceless gold bar that for most people would remain unattainable ILLUSTRATION 163. This image may have reminded people of the Benson and Hedges tobacco advertisement of the previous decade (Vaknin, 2007, p.95). In the 'You can take a White Horse anywhere' campaign, the settings became ever more original ILLUSTRATION 164.

Worth its weight in Chivas Regal.

ILLUSTRATION 163
1986

ILLUSTRATION 164
1981

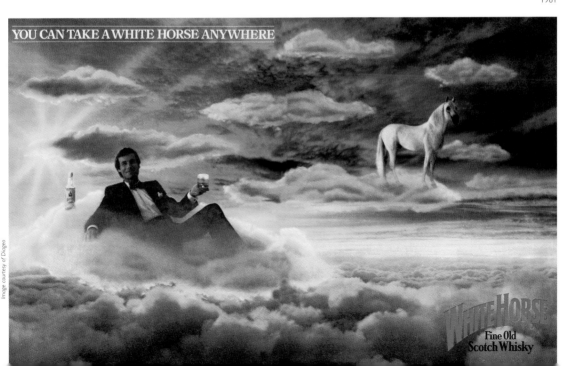

YOU CAN TAKE A WHITE HORSE ANYWHERE

White Horse
Fine Old
Scotch Whisky

There's an art in picking the right one.

To the palate of the true connoisseur, there is nothing quite like Martini's unique combination of the choicest wines and herbs. It is inimitable. Irresistible. And absolutely right.

ILLUSTRATION 165

Telegraph Sunday Magazine, 1982

ILLUSTRATION 166

1981

Campari: simply a matter of good taste.

Campari and Soda: Campari, ice and a splash of soda to taste. Negroni: 1/3 Campari, 1/3 Gin, 1/3 Red Vermouth, ice. Shake then strain into cocktail glass. Add slice of orange. Americano: 1/2 Campari, 1/2 Red Vermouth. A squeeze of lemon rind, cracked ice.

In line with the industry's voluntary advertising codes, advertisements continued to use indirect methods of indicating their brand's superiority. One common technique was the association of precious luxuries with the attributes of an alcoholic product. Martini's 'the right one' is included in the headline of this advertisement ILLUSTRATION 165 in which the unique golden grapes represent the vermouth. A large step away from these codes is a Campari advertisement, which suggests that a glass of Campari after a good day's skiing ILLUSTRATION 166 may enhance your physical and possibly sexual capabilities. The placement of this advertisement in a January issue of *Time* magazine targets those able to afford to go skiing at this time of year.

As with cosmetics advertising, film stars were sometimes used to promote alcoholic products, such as this example for Bacardi rum ILLUSTRATION 167. The code's principle of not implying that alcohol boosts sexual success or attractiveness is completely ignored here. Telly Savalas, successful star of the television series *Kojak*, is being observed by an elegant woman at the bar and the phrase 'forbidden fruit' has an obvious double meaning.

The association of a drink with luxury can be seen in this special offer, for Gordon's gin, of a chance to win a flight on Concorde. Concorde had first flown ten years earlier but was still the ultimate in luxury travel ILLUSTRATION 168. It was worth buying the Gordon's brand, which had by the Eighties become the world's best-selling gin, to stand a chance of winning such a prize.

ILLUSTRATION 167

1984

ILLUSTRATION 168

Telegraph Sunday Magazine, 1987

"Well, they said anything could happen."

ILLUSTRATION 169
1982

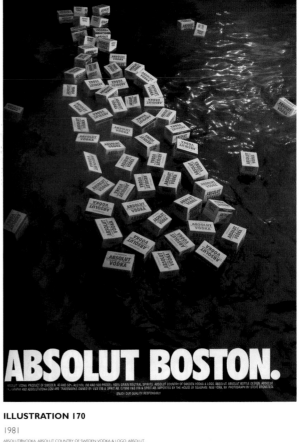

ABSOLUT BOSTON.

ABSOLUT VODKA. PRODUCT OF SWEDEN. 40 AND 50% ALC/VOL (80 AND 100 PROOF). 100% GRAIN NEUTRAL SPIRITS. ABSOLUT, COUNTRY OF SWEDEN VODKA & LOGO, ABSOLUT, ABSOLUT BOTTLE DESIGN, ABSOLUT CALLIGRAPH AND ABSOLUTVODKA.COM ARE TRADEMARKS OWNED BY V&S VIN & SPRIT AB. ©1998 V&S VIN & SPRIT AB. IMPORTED BY THE HOUSE OF SEAGRAM, NEW YORK, NY. PHOTOGRAPH BY STEVE BRONSTEIN.
ENJOY OUR QUALITY RESPONSIBLY.

ILLUSTRATION 170
1981

ABSOLUT®VODKA. ABSOLUT COUNTRY OF SWEDEN VODKA & LOGO, ABSOLUT,
ABSOLUT BOTTLE DESIGN AND ABSOLUT CALLIGRAPHY ARE TRADEMARKS
OWNED BY V&S VIN & SPRIT AB (publ). ©2006 V&S VIN & SPRIT AB (publ)

Many other alcohol companies continued with their successful campaigns into the 1980s. Smirnoff stuck with its 'well, they said anything could happen' campaign ILLUSTRATION 169, the advertisements getting more and more strange. Johnny Weissmuller, star of the early Tarzan films, swings out of the film to sweep up a woman much to the astonishment of the cinema audience.

However, in the Eighties there was a new brand of vodka. Absolut vodka, competitor of Smirnoff, burst on to the advertising scene in 1981 with one of the most innovative, imaginative and witty advertising campaigns, by TBWA, which would go on to win hundreds of awards. The main purpose of the campaign was to build a healthy and lasting brand for this Swedish vodka in the American market dominated by its own brands. Unlike other spirits, Absolut comes in an unusual squat bottle inspired by Swedish medicine bottles. Another original feature of the bottle is that it has no label, the product information being printed directly in colourful lettering onto the glass.

TBWA's campaign cleverly used just the brand name with only one other word, making no attempt to demonstrate how Absolut should be drunk. Although Absolut advertising campaigns were only launched in Europe in 1992 (and so will be mentioned again in the

ILLUSTRATION 171
She, 1982

next chapter) a couple of examples are shown here. The campaign was launched with Absolut Boston as the first in the 'cities' series **ILLUSTRATION 170** in which the shape of the bottle is outlined in boxes of Absolut, associating it with the Boston Tea Party.[11]

In 1985 with sales of Absolut growing, an original, innovative advertising technique was used in Absolut's series of 'Art' advertisements. The first of these was a painting by Andy Warhol. Before then, advertisers had not considered using original fine art as a promotional tool. The campaign was an immediate success. Never a company to rest on its laurels, Absolut developed a range of flavoured vodkas which were advertised at the end of the Eighties using the image of lemon peel in the shape of the bottle and a pun on the word 'appeal'.

Babycham also continued to advertise in women's magazines. This 1982 advertisement is from *She* magazine **ILLUSTRATION 171**. The 'I'd love' slogan has been dropped in favour of the imperative, 'love a Babycham', whilst the

11 In 1773, American colonists took direct action against British rule by throwing crates of tea overboard in Boston Harbour in protest against increased taxation.

Nectar

ILLUSTRATION 172

Country Life, 1981

IT'S ABOUT AS LIKELY AS A DUFF BOTTLE OF HIRONDELLE.

For some years now, Hirondelle has enjoyed the reputation of being a consistently good table wine.

These days, with the proliferation of unfamiliar wines on the market, it pays even more to know exactly what it is you're buying.

Maintaining the quality of wine will always be a delicate business. Not only great care and skill are needed. It also takes years of experience.

Hedges & Butler, who select and ship Hirondelle, have that experience. They've been wine merchants since 1667.

That's why they're confident about Hirondelle.

Confident enough to guarantee every bottle.

Hirondelle is available in red, sweet white, medium-dry white and rosé.

ILLUSTRATION 173
1980s

red lips suggest the social and sexual attractiveness of the product's drinkers. Like the simple Absolut message, the taste of Drambuie is summed up in one word, 'nectar', as here ILLUSTRATION 172 where a humming bird drinks the liqueur.

According to a study carried out in 1988, beer and wine had swapped places. Against falling beer consumption, wine drinking rose from 17.9 pints per head per annum in 1980 to 25.9 pints per head per annum in 1987 (Burnett, 1999, p.154). Blue Nun and Mateus Rosé were still popular but another brand had joined the stable of relatively inexpensive European wines, namely Hirondelle. A humorous 1980s advertisement uses an image

representing the well-known English phrase 'raining cats and dogs' to emphasise the impossibility of a 'duff bottle' of Hirondelle ILLUSTRATION 173.

The end of the Eighties saw the establishment of the Portman Group of leading British drinks producers, whose main aim was to promote sensible drinking, especially amongst young people, through voluntary codes. Under its influence and that of the Advertising Standards Authority (ASA), the drinks advertising industry has begun to regulate the contents of its campaigns – though some of the advertisements from the 1990s show no evidence of adhering to these codes, probably because they still remained voluntary.

Chapter 8

Wine, women…

During the early part of the 1990s, 'advertisers detected a distinct shift in consumer values and attitudes. The 1980s' accent on materialism and individualism was fading fast and being replaced by a less superficial, more considered mood… Substance was in. Veneer out.' (Davies, 1998, p.224) Consumers had become increasingly aware of the dangers to health of excessive binge-drinking, through government campaigns, and the rise in the incidence of alcohol abuse and underage drinking. The price of alcohol had fallen in proportion to people's disposable income, which some argued was a stronger factor in the growth of alcohol consumption than expensive advertising campaigns. Many companies and their advertisers increasingly flaunted the voluntary codes governing alcohol advertising. The arrival and exponential growth of the Internet in the mid-Nineties had an impact on advertising in printed media just as television advertising had initially affected print advertising in the 1950s.

In 1997, Guinness alone spent ten million pounds on advertising. This may have led to it achieving its highest percentage share of the British beer market, 5.2 per cent, which by the end of the century was dominated by lager at sixty-six per cent. Following on from the successful 'Pure Genius' campaign, Ogilvy & Mather launched its Guinness black and white 'fractionals' campaign. These were supposed to be the doodlings of the man with a Guinness and were used in a variety of media, including print. The images in **ILLUSTRATION 174** resemble anyone's

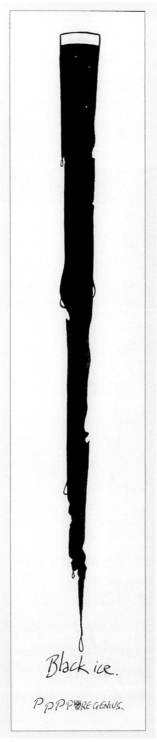

Black ice.

P.P.P. PURE GENIUS.

Image courtesy of Diageo

ILLUSTRATION 174

1992

It's not easy drinking in space..

GUINNESS

PURE GENIUS.

Image courtesy of Diageo

Is it St. Patrick's Day, or am I seeing things?

PURE GENIUS.

Image courtesy of Diageo

ILLUSTRATION 175

1995

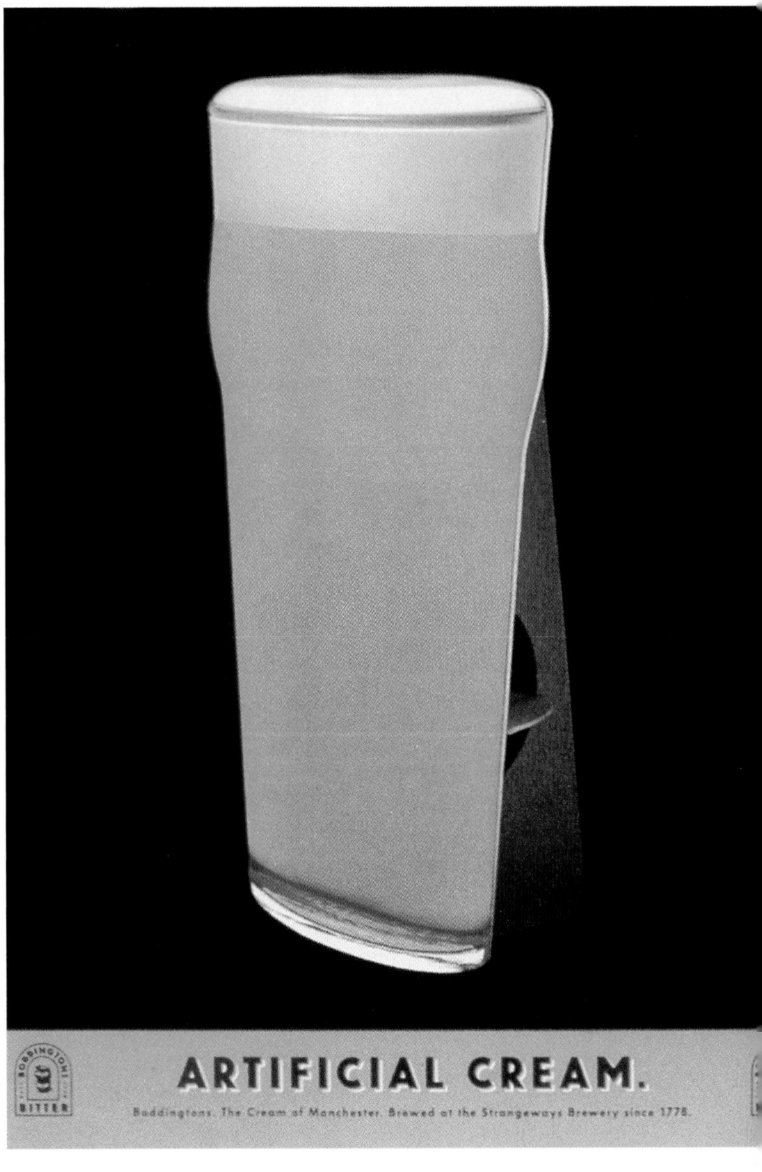

ILLUSTRATION 176

1995

ILLUSTRATION 177

1995

doodles whilst **ILLUSTRATION 175** shows how their simplicity could be used topically, as in this newspaper advertisement related to the main tennis story.

Towards the end of the century, in its advertising campaign for Whitbread's Boddingtons bitter, Bartle Bogle Hegarty used various humorous visual devices to show the creaminess of the beer in unusual ways, and thus differentiate it from the other beer products on the market. One presented Boddingtons as an ice-cream cone, another **ILLUSTRATION 176** as a cardboard replica.

Between 1994 and 1999, twenty-five per cent of the 4.5 billion litres of lager sold in Britain were of canned lager, mainly for home consumption. Though there was now a prolific choice of brands, including Indian brands such as Kingfisher and Cobra (brewed in Britain since 1997), European lagers held their own. Despite these vast sales figures, the aim of all the beer companies was to keep their customers brand loyal in this crowded market.

An advertisement for Carlsberg's Skol lager by the Leagas Shafron Davis Ayer agency uses a punning device to link the hops used to brew lager with the hops of a 1970s toy in an appeal to nostalgia **ILLUSTRATION 177**. At the same time, Heineken was using part of a famous Van Gogh painting, both to commemorate the centenary of the painter's death in 1889 and to continue its long

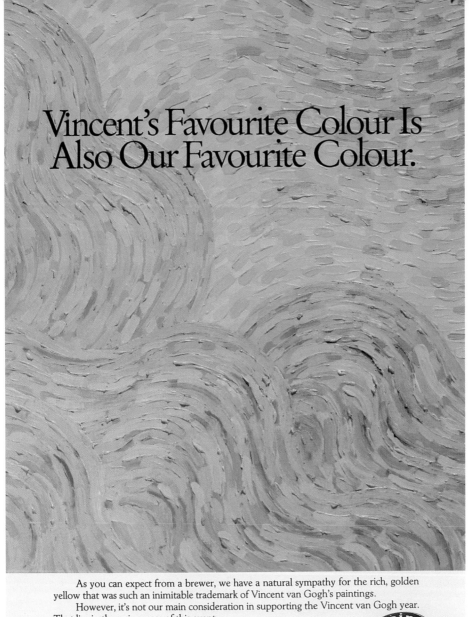

Vincent's Favourite Colour Is Also Our Favourite Colour.

As you can expect from a brewer, we have a natural sympathy for the rich, golden yellow that was such an inimitable trademark of Vincent van Gogh's paintings.

However, it's not our main consideration in supporting the Vincent van Gogh year. That lies in the uniqueness of this event.

From the 30th of March until the 29th of July nearly all of Van Gogh's masterpieces will come together in Amsterdam.

A monumentous reunion that probably can't be repeated ever again. What more reason did we need?

ILLUSTRATION 178
1990

association with its Dutch homeland **ILLUSTRATION 178**. This was also designed to appeal to better-educated consumers who could recognise the painting.

Partly as a response to continued government promotion of responsible drinking and anti-drink driving campaigns, and partly through its identification of a niche

ILLUSTRATION 179

1995

ILLUSTRATION 180

GQ, 1991

market, Guinness launched a new product in the mid Eighties – Kaliber beer, the first alcohol free lager. The comedian Billy Connolly fronted the campaign because, as well as being a famous personality, he was known to be a reformed drinker **ILLUSTRATION 179**. The strapline cleverly makes the point that if you drink Kaliber beer, you will remember the night before.

Throughout the Nineties, despite many whisky brands having become household names, there was a slow decline in whisky consumption. This led to the companies having to balance the retention of the traditional consumer market of forty-plus males against attracting younger drinkers, who preferred other spirits, especially vodka. Dewar's, which consistently emphasised its quality in all its advertising, appears in two advertisements to be targeting these two diverse sectors of the market. In the first **ILLUSTRATION 180**, the emphasis is on the traditional Scottish 'water of life', whilst in the second sexual attraction is being blatantly used to entice younger

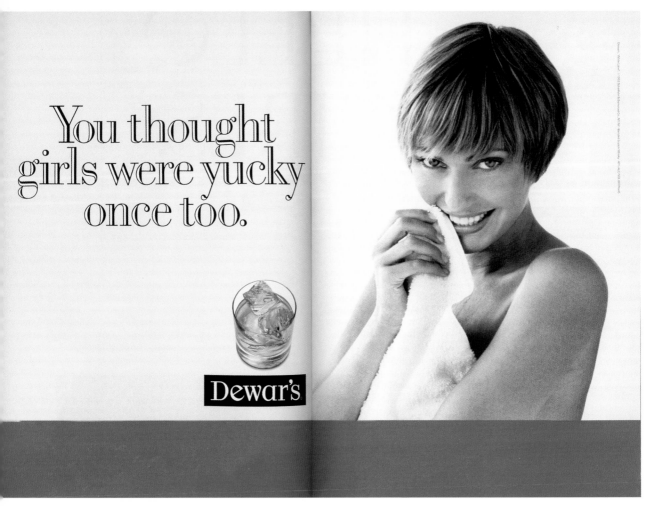

You thought girls were yucky once too.

Dewar's

ILLUSTRATION 181

GQ, 1995

drinkers to purchase the product **ILLUSTRATION 181**. Surprisingly, this advertisement appears to be clearly breaking the voluntary code not to show images of people who are, or look, under twenty-five years of age.

Other whisky companies continued the tradition of emphasising the taste of their brands in their advertising campaigns. Chivas Regal appears to have broken away from the stereotypical look of advertisements by experimenting with a more editorial style **ILLUSTRATION 182**. On the other hand, this advertisement for Johnnie Walker Red Label adheres to stereotypes, showing two older, very well-dressed women enjoying their evening out drinking the product, the taste referring to their fashionable outfits and expensive jewellery **ILLUSTRATION 183**. Another advertisement for the better-known Black Label brand is aimed clearly at the younger market (i.e. the under twenty-fives as graduates)

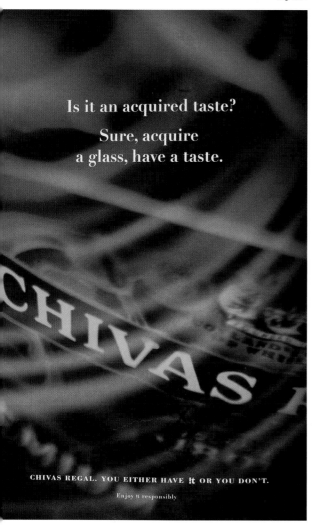

Thank Dad for putting you in the Black.

Ultimately, there's Black.

Image courtesy of Diageo

ILLUSTRATION 184

GQ, 1992

using a visual wordplay on black – a student graduating in black cap and gown and Black Label whisky – to celebrate the event **ILLUSTRATION 184**. J&B blended Scotch whisky, by now second only to Dewar's in market sales, very successfully advertised itself through a series of creatively witty advertisements such as **ILLUSTRATION 185** showing its distinctive J&B brand on a crowded bar of music.

ILLUSTRATION 185

GQ, 1991

J&B in a crowded bar.

J&B Scotch Whisky. Blended and bottled in Scotland by Justerini & Brooks, fine wine and spirit merchants since 1749.

Image courtesy of Diageo

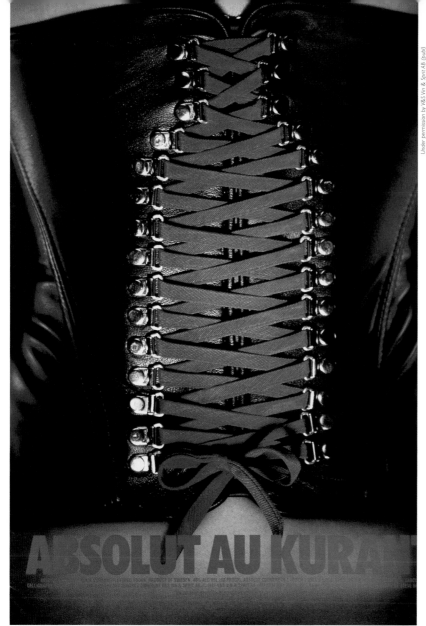

ABSOLUT AU KURANT

ILLUSTRATION 186

GQ, 1999

By the start of the Nineties, Absolut's sales were soaring and the advertisements were not only becoming famous but winning prestigious awards. Absolut launched in Europe in 1992, with TBWA employing the same successful 'cities' format used in the earlier American campaign, namely Absolut Venice. Wheat was laid out early in St Marks Square in Venice in a bottle shape and the photographer took the shot as the pigeons descended onto the square. Another flavoured Absolut was launched the same year, as can be seen in a sexier advertisement **ILLUSTRATION 186** where the bottle is shaped as a woman's corset ready for untying.

ILLUSTRATION 187

GQ, 1991

ILLUSTRATION 188

GQ, 1995

ILLUSTRATION 189

GQ, 1995

Smirnoff's sales had been adversely affected by the arrival of Absolut in the Eighties. In this decade, the company tried to reverse the trend by changing its party image to one of clean family living. It spent more than five million pounds on its advertising campaign with its new slogan of 'Home is where you find it' **ILLUSTRATION 187**. Three young people wearing Groucho Marx[12] false noses and glasses for comic effect are in a bar having a good time. One has the feeling that it was not an entirely successful campaign as a few years later Smirnoff launched its 'pure' campaign using the word 'pure' with one other word – a concept remarkably similar to its competitor Absolut's two-word slogans **ILLUSTRATION 188**.

After years of successful advertising, Bacardi had become the world's most popular brand of rum. In its 'just add Bacardi' series, which stressed its long history as a mixer, a shot of Bacardi being poured is transformed into a woman swimming through a sea that is also a city skyline **ILLUSTRATION 189**. In a later advertisement the slogan pokes fun at the politically correct language and social

12 Groucho Marx (1890–1977), American comedian and film star whose trademarks were fake eyebrows, a moustache, glasses and a cigar.

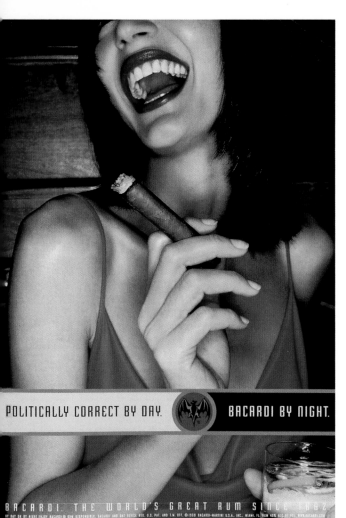

POLITICALLY CORRECT BY DAY. BACARDI BY NIGHT.

BACARDI. THE WORLD'S GREAT RUM SINCE 1862.

ILLUSTRATION 190
GQ, 1999

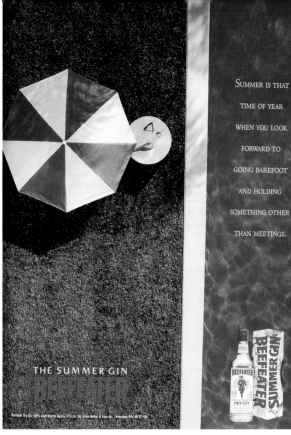

SUMMER IS THAT TIME OF YEAR WHEN YOU LOOK FORWARD TO GOING BAREFOOT AND HOLDING SOMETHING OTHER THAN MEETINGS.

THE SUMMER GIN
BEEFEATER

ILLUSTRATION 191
GQ, 1992

behaviour of the Nineties **ILLUSTRATION 190**. An independent-looking woman, out having a drink of Bacardi after work, is smoking a cigar. This would have fallen foul of UK legislation restricting tobacco advertising, but was allowed in America where this advertisement originates. The suggestion is that Bacardi could turn you into a socially successful woman.

Spirit companies no longer targeted advertising campaigns only at the Christmas market but also increasingly at the summer market. Here, Beefeater gin is recommended as perfect for enjoying on holiday **ILLUSTRATION 191**.

In **ILLUSTRATION 192** the high-quality luxury product Remy Martin brandy takes a phrase common amongst courting couples and adds a dollop of visual humour. The drink is thus associated with a place on a pedestal, showing that it should be treated with the respect and reverence it deserves.

Want to come up for
a drink sometime?

REMY MARTIN

Remy Martin Fine Champagne cognac. Exclusively
from grapes of the Cognac region's two best areas.

ILLUSTRATION 192
GQ, 1995

BAILEYS

AN EVENING TO REFLECT ON.

BAILEYS
ORIGINAL IRISH CREAM
ORIGINAL IRISH CREAM

ILLUSTRATION 193
GQ, 1991

Two liqueurs which came into their own in advertising terms in the Eighties and Nineties were Baileys Irish cream liqueur and Grand Marnier triple sec, neither of which had been affected by the drop in consumption of other spirits. Baileys Irish cream liqueur, created in 1974 from a blend of Irish whiskey and cream, was drunk by more women than men in all social classes, and mainly at home. Baileys' advertising agency spent more than thirty million dollars on its advertising in Europe. This did result in it becoming the leader in the cream liqueur market, but its advertising budget was out of all proportion to the actual number of cases sold. Although consistent advertising is said to maintain brand loyalty, the Baileys brand regularly changed its themes, as in this example – Baileys Irish cream liqueur at home after a night out **ILLUSTRATION 193**. This does not appear to have affected its sales in any way.

Grand Marnier, *slightly* less mysterious than love.

ILLUSTRATION 194
GQ, 1995

Grand Marnier, especially served with ice, gained in popularity in this decade, partly through its inventive advertising campaigns. A 1995 series of advertisements are all based on the theme of mystery and love, in surreal colourful evocative 'love' settings **ILLUSTRATION 194**.

A brand new development in the mid Nineties were the brightly coloured, flavoured alcoholic beverages (FABs), tasting strongly of fruit juice rather than alcohol, that are now more popularly known now as 'alcopops'. Some cynically believe that they were developed by the alcohol

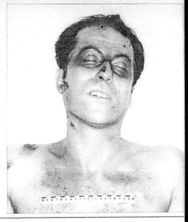

THIS IS AN ADVERTISEMENT FOR ORANGE JUICE.

🙂 **VAUXHALL** If you're drinking this Christmas please don't drive.

ILLUSTRATION 195
1990s

ILLUSTRATION 196
1999

companies with the sole aim of targeting the teenage market. Alcopops were blamed for increasing teenage drinking by focusing the advertising on youth and fun, which some thought resulted in the establishment of the habit of drinking alcohol from a very young age. Much research on this subject has since been done and the arguments continue into this century. However, since 1996, the voluntary advertising codes have been strengthened to discourage alcohol producers from targeting the under 18s. An early product was Hooper's Hooch, which was launched with virtually no advertising but by 1996 had gained seventy per cent of this market. The most popular and easily recognisable brands among young people nowadays are Smirnoff Ice, Bacardi Breezer and WKD.

As Britain approached the new millennium, the government took the opportunity to increase its promotion of anti-drink driving campaigns. These two advertisements, **ILLUSTRATIONS 195 and 196**, graphically get their messages across.

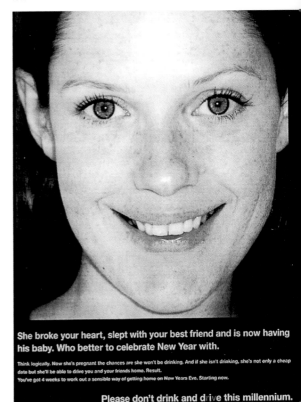

She broke your heart, slept with your best friend and is now having his baby. Who better to celebrate New Year with.

Think logically. Now she's pregnant the chances are she won't be drinking. And if she isn't drinking, she's not only a cheap date but she'll be able to drive you and your friends home. Result.

You've got 4 weeks to work out a sensible way of getting home on New Years Eve. Starting now.

Please don't drink and drive this millennium.

It's time for a change to Gallo.

Grilled Norwegian salmon on a lattice of green beans.
©E.&J. Gallo Winery, Modesto, CA.

ILLUSTRATION 197
GQ, 1991

The advertisement of wine in the Nineties remained a small percentage of the total alcohol advertising market in Britain. New wines from Australia, New Zealand, South Africa and America were now competing with the traditional European wines, as in this advertisement for Gallo, showing the strong relationship between food and wine **ILLUSTRATION 197**.

In this current century, advertisers of alcoholic products are coming under increased pressure to abide by the voluntary codes. Many think these should now be made compulsory as happened with tobacco advertising.

Although drinks companies do require date of birth for entry to their Internet sites, there is nothing to stop young people faking their age and logging on. So restricting or even banning alcoholic drinks advertisements in print will have little or no impact as anyone can access information about alcohol on the Internet. Just as some of the best advertising campaigns arose out of the ban on tobacco advertising, Paul Arden believes that 'restrictions on alcohol advertising will put work back on track and make it intelligent and clever again. I see it as a real challenge for creative people.' (Carson, 2004, p.66)

RULES GOVERNING ALCOHOL ADVERTISING

THESE RULES ARE BASED ON A NUMBER OF CORE PRINCIPLES AND PROHIBIT ANY ADVERTISING WHICH:

- **Targets young people under the age of 18**
  - ☐ markets alcoholic drinks to under-18s,
  - ☐ incorporates images of people who are, or look as if they are, under twenty-five years of age

- **Implies that alcohol can make you more popular, successful, attractive etc.**
  - ☐ suggests that alcohol is essential to social success, popularity and acceptance
  - ☐ suggests that drinking can contribute to sexual success or attractiveness
  - ☐ implies that the successful outcome of a social occasion is dependent on the consumption of alcohol
  - ☐ suggests that drinking can overcome boredom, loneliness or other problems or that drinking can bring about a change in mood
  - ☐ suggests that drinking can enhance mental, physical or sexual capabilities
  - ☐ implies that people who drink alcohol are brave, tough or daring

- **Encourages irresponsible drinking habits**
  - ☐ portrays alcohol being drunk in situations where this may be unsafe – e.g. driving, swimming or using machinery
  - ☐ shows alcohol being drunk in a work environment
  - ☐ links alcohol with aggressive, dangerous, irresponsible or antisocial behaviour
  - ☐ encourages excessive or binge-drinking
  - ☐ suggests that drinking is an essential part of daily routine

- **Suggests any association with, acceptance of, or allusion to illicit drugs**

- **Promotes the alcoholic strength of a drink (although the alcoholic nature of the drink must be communicated in its packaging)**

(From page iii of *Acquire – Alcohol Concern's Quarterly Information and Research Bulletin*, Autumn 2003, pull-out report, www.alcoholconcern.org.uk)

ABSOLUT – Lars Olsson Smith produced this Swedish vodka in 1879 using a new distillation method. Product launched early 1980s in America and 1992 in Europe. Owned by the V&S Group until acquired by Pernod Ricard in 2008.

ALCOPOPS – flavoured alcoholic beverages, to which various fruit juices or other flavourings have been added. Appeared first in the mid 1990s.

ALLSOPP – English brewery. Produced India Pale ale for export to the British Empire from 1822 until 1959. The Allsopp name was dropped in 1959 and in 1971 Ind Coope was incorporated into Allied Breweries. (See Ind Coope)

BABYCHAM – light sparkling pear drink invented by Francis Showering and launched in 1953. Popular in the 1960s and 1970s. Brand now owned by Constellation Europe.

BACARDI – the world's largest privately held, family-owned spirits company and producer of rums, founded in Cuba in 1862. After the 1959 Cuban revolution, the company moved its base to the Bahamas. Diversified into mixer drinks such as Bacardi Breezers in the 1980s. Now the Bacardi Martini company.

BAILEYS – liqueur created in 1974 from a blend of cream and Irish whiskey. Popular drink with ice and the number one liqueur in the world. Now a Diageo brand.

BALLANTINE'S – blended Scotch whisky first produced by George Ballantine in 1827 in Edinburgh. Brand acquired by Pernod Ricard in 2005.

BARRETT'S – nineteenth-century London brewery famous for its stouts. Company no longer exists.

BASS – brewery founded by William Bass in 1777 in Burton-on-Trent. In 1967 merged with Charrington United Breweries becoming Bass Charrington in 1983, with ownership passing from InBev to Coors at the beginning of this century. Famous red triangle logo.

BEEFEATER – London dry gin brand produced and distributed by Pernod Ricard.

BELL'S – whisky company established in 1825. Arthur Bell's name was not added to the brand until 1895. Now owned by Diageo.

BLACK & WHITE – blended Scotch whisky first produced by James Buchanan, who devised the logo in 1895. After several mergers and acquisitions the brand is now owned by Diageo.

BLUE NUN – sweet German wine launched in Mainz in 1923 by the H. Sichel Söhne Company. Brand popular in the 1970s. Founding company purchased by Langguth in 1996.

BODDINGTONS – brewery founded in 1778 in Manchester. The brand was taken over by Whitbread in 1989 but is now owned by InBev.

BOOTH'S – London dry gin distillery founded by the Booth family about 1740. Another Diageo brand.

BUCHANAN'S – blended Scotch whisky produced in 1884 by James Buchanan. The brand is now owned by Diageo.

BULMERS – English west country cider company founded in 1887 by Percy Bulmer. Granted royal warrant in 1911. HP Bulmer Ltd is now the world's largest cider maker.

CAMPARI – bitter Italian aperitif made in Milan since 1860. Still owned by the Campari Group.

CARLING – beer first brewed in Canada during the American years of prohibition and in Britain in 1964. Became the first draught lager in 1965. In 1999 was the first company to achieve sales of one billion pints in the United Kingdom. Brand now belongs to Coors.

CARLSBERG – Danish brewery founded in 1847. Merged with Tuborg in 1970 to form United Breweries and then became Carlsberg CV in 1987. More than 80 per cent of its lager sales are outside Denmark.

CASTLEMAINE XXXX – Australian lager brand launched in 1924 and now brewed under licence in the United Kingdom by InBev.

CHIVAS REGAL – whisky distillery founded in 1801 by the Chivas brothers in Aberdeen, Scotland. Brand acquired by Pernod Ricard in 2000.

CINZANO – Italian vermouth made from fortified wine flavoured with aromatic herbs and spices. Brand has been part of the Campari Group since 1999.

COORS – American brewing company founded in 1873. In 2002 Coors acquired Bass from InBev and is now the UK's second largest brewer with brands including Worthington and Carling.

CUTTY SARK – blended whisky brand launched in 1923 by Berry Brothers and still owned by Berry Brothers and Rudd Ltd.

DEWAR'S – blended Scotch whisky company founded by John Dewar in Perth in 1846. Brand now part of Bacardi Martini Ltd.

DIAGEO – the world's largest multinational beer, wine and spirits company. The company was formed in 1997 from the merger of Guinness and Grand Metropolitan and is listed on the London Stock Exchange.

DOUBLE DIAMOND – pale ale brewed since 1876 by Ind Coope in Burton-on-Trent. Company became part of Allied breweries in 1961 and in 1993 merged with Carlsberg, which still owns the brand.

DRAMBUIE – Scotland's liqueur dating back to 1745 in Skye. Made from malt and grain whiskies and flavourings. Still owned by the Mackinnon family but now produced near Edinburgh.

DRY SACK – Spanish sherry brand of Williams and Humbert.

DUBONNET – red French aperitif created by Joseph Dubonnet in 1846. Brand owned by the Pernod Ricard group.

(THE) FAMOUS GROUSE – blended Scotch whisky first produced in 1897 by Matthew Gloag and Sons Ltd. In 1970 the company was sold to Highland Distilleries before becoming part of the Edrington Group, in turn owned by the Robertson Trust, in 1999.

GALLO – Californian red and white wines produced by E. & J. Gallo Winery, which remains a family owned company.

GILBEY'S – London dry gin. Walter and Alfred Gilbey established a gin distillery in London in 1851. Diageo brand.

GORDON'S – gin first distilled by Alexander Gordon in 1769 in London. Brand leader among London gins. Green bottle brand bought in 1985 by Guinness plc but subsequently acquired by Diageo.

GRAND MARNIER – liqueur created in France in 1880 by Alexandre Marnier-Lapostolle. Brand still owned by the Grand Marnier Company.

GRANT'S – blended Scotch whisky first produced in 1887 by William Grant. William Grant and Sons Ltd remains an independent family distillery.

GUINNESS – company founded in 1759 in Dublin. Stout first brewed in London in 1936. Now owned by Diageo.

HAIG – blended Scotch whisky launched by John Haig in 1824. Diageo brand.

HEINEKEN – lager brewed in the Netherlands since 1864. Company renamed Heineken N.V. in 1968.

HENNESSY – French brandy since 1765. Leading brand distributed by Diageo on behalf of Moët Hennessy.

HIGHLAND QUEEN – blended Scotch whisky first produced by Roderick Macdonald around 1893. Brand now owned by Glenmorangie Company Ltd.

INBEV – the world's leading brewing multinational company with headquarters in Belgium. Owns many famous British brands such as Bass and those formerly belonging to Whitbread.

IND COOPE – brewery originally based in Romford, Essex. Became part of Allied Breweries in 1961, merging with Carlsberg in 1993. (See Allsopp)

J&B – blended Scotch whisky. Distillery founded in 1749 by Giacomo Justerini and George Johnson. It became J&B when Alfred Brooks bought in to the company. Diageo brand.

JOHN SMITH'S – brewery in Tadcaster, Yorkshire since 1884. Now owned by Heineken. Considered the number one bitter brand in the UK.

JOHNNIE WALKER – blended Scotch whisky company founded in 1820 by John Walker. This brand named in 1908. Guinness Distillers acquired the brand in 1925 but it is now owned by Diageo.

KALIBER – alcohol free lager launched in 1987 by Guinness. Now a Diageo brand.

LANSON – champagne company founded in 1760 by François Delamotte, who went in to partnership with Jean-Baptiste Lanson. Company changed its name in 1837.

LONDON DRY GIN – well known perfumed gin. Does not have to be distilled in London.

LONG JOHN – blended Scotch whisky produced in the Tormore Distillery owned by Pernod Ricard.

LONG LIFE – beer brewed by Ind Coope, now part of Carlsberg.

MACKESON – stout brewed in Hythe, England from 1907. Used as a tonic for invalids and nursing mothers. Known as a 'milk' stout until the term was banned in 1946. Whitbread owned it before InBev bought the company in 2000.

MARTELL – cognac house founded in 1715. Brand now owned by Pernod Ricard.

MARTINI – vermouth by Martini & Rossi based in Turin. Associated with James Bond films. Part of Bacardi Martini Group.

MATEUS ROSÉ – rosé wine from Portugal very popular in Britain in the Sixties and Seventies. Owned by Sogrape Vinhos.

MILD BITTER – was the main ale in England until the 1960s. Traditionally a working man's drink.

MOËT & CHANDON – French champagne launched in 1743 and distributed by Diageo on behalf of Moët Hennessy.

PERNOD – French pastis produced by Henri Pernod from 1915, when straight absinthe was banned. A Pernod Ricard brand.

PERNOD RICARD – global producer of wine and spirits formed from a merger of the two companies in 1974. It is France's largest supplier and distributor of aniseed drinks.

PIMM'S – alcohol based fruit cup created by James Pimm in the 1820s. Exact ingredients remain secret. Associated with English summers. Brand owned by Diageo.

PIPER HEIDSIECK – French champagne house founded in 1785 by Florens-Louis Heidsieck and combined with the name Piper in 1839. Now part of Rémy Cointreau Group.

RÉMY MARTIN – French cognac house established in 1724. Became part of the Rémy Cointreau Group in 1991.

SANDEMAN – port sold by Scotsman George Sandeman in London in 1790. Famous Don figure drawn by artist George Massiot Brown in 1928 and still used as logo. Member of the Sogrape Group but distributed by Pernod Ricard.

SCOTTISH & NEWCASTLE (S&N) – large multinational brewing company taken over in 2008 by Carlsberg and Heineken.

SKOL – lager with a continental name launched by Ind Coope in 1960.

SMIRNOFF – Russian vodka first distilled in Moscow in 1864. American rights to brand sold in 1934 to Heublein and acquired by Grand Metropolitan plc in 1988. Now a Diageo brand.

TEACHER'S – blended whisky first sold by William Teacher in 1830. Brand owned now by Beam Global UK Ltd.

TENNENT'S – first lager brewed in Scotland in 1885 and first canned lager in 1936. InBev brand.

TRUMAN'S – English brewery founded in seventeenth century in Brick Lane, London and closed in 1988. The building is now an arts and events centre.

VAT 69 – blended Scotch whisky launched in 1882 by Sanderson. Brand owned by Diageo.

WATNEY'S – Red Barrel keg beer first brewed in 1931 in London. Very popular brand in the 1960s but now brewed abroad for the overseas markets.

WHITBREAD – English brewery founded in 1742 in London and closed in 1976. Company concentrates now on the leisure sector.

WHITE HORSE – blended Scotch whisky launched in 1890s and named after one of the Edinburgh coaching inns.

WORTHINGTON – ales first brewed in 1866. Company merged with Bass in 1927. White Shield brand re-launched in 2002 and owned by Coors.

BIBLIOGRAPHY

ALCOHOL CONCERN, *Acquire: Alcohol Concern's Information and Research Bulletin*, Autumn 2003, No. 38, pp.i–vii

AUSTIN, Erica Weintraub, 'Why advertisers and researchers should focus on media literacy to respond to the effect of alcohol advertising on youth', *International Journal of Advertising*, 2006, Vol. 25, Issue 4, pp.541–44

BELK, Russell W. and Richard W. POLLAY, 'Images of ourselves: the good life in twentieth century advertising', *Journal of Consumer Research*, Vol. 11, March 1985, pp.887–97

BENADY, David, 'High spirits', *Designweek*, Vol. 21, part 2, March 2006, pp.16–17

BURNETT, John (1999) *Liquid pleasure: a social history of drink in modern Britain*, Routledge

BURTENSHAW, Ken, Nick MARLOW and Caroline BARFOOT (2006) *The fundamentals of creative advertising*, Ava

CAMNITZER, Luis, 'Absolut relativity', *Third text*, Vol. 38, Spring 1997, pp.86–91

CARSON, Paula, 'Half-empty or half-full?', *Creative Review*, Dec. 2004, pp.65–6

DAVIES, Jim (1998) *The book of Guinness advertising*, Guinness Publishing

DAVIS, Melisa (2005) *More than a name: an introduction to branding*, Aval

DYER, Gillian (1982) *Advertising as communication*, Methuen

ENCYCLOPEDIA of consumer brands (1994) Vol. 1, St. James Press

FISHER, Joseph C. (1993) *Advertising alcohol consumption and abuse: a worldwide survey*, Greenwood Press

GOBE, Marc (2001) *Emotional branding: the new paradigm for connecting brands to people*, Allworth Press

GRIFFITHS, Marc (2005) *Guinness is Guinness: the colourful story of a black and white brand*, Cyan Books

LEWIS, Richard W. (1996) *Absolut book: the Absolut vodka advertising story*, Journey Editions

LURY, Giles (2001) *Brandwatching: lifting the lid on branding*, 2nd revised and enlarged edition, Blackhall Publishing

MCLUHAN, Marshall (1964) Understanding Media, Routledge & Kegan Paul

MELLORS, Tim, 'Fags 'n' booze', *Creative Review*, Dec. 2002, pp.47–50

MYERSON, Jeremy (2002) *Rewind: 40 years of design and advertising*, Phaidon Press

NELSON, Jon P., 'Alcohol advertising in magazines: do beer, wine and spirits advertisements target youth?' *Contemporary Economic Policy*, Vol. 24, No. 3, July 2006, pp.357–69

NEVETT, R. (1982) *Advertising in Britain*, Heinemann

OXFORD BROOKES UNIVERSITY, National Brewing Library and Archives

POLLAY, Richard W., 'The subsidising sizzle: a descriptive history of print advertising 1900–1960', *Journal of Marketing*, Vol. 49, Summer 1985, pp.24–37

PROTZ, Roger and Tony MILLNS (editors) (1992) *Called to the bar: an account of the first 21 years of the Campaign for Real Ale*, CAMRA

PROTZ, Roger (1995) *The ultimate encyclopedia of beer*, Carlton/Prion

RUSSELL, Iain, Scottish Brewing Archive

SIBLEY, Brian (1985) *The book of Guinness advertising*, Guinness Books

WALTON, Stuart and Brian GLOVER (2006) *The illustrated encyclopedia of wine, beer and spirits*, Lorenz